T0326726

THE
60
SECOND
SALE

THE
ULTIMATE SYSTEM
FOR
BUILDING
LIFELONG CLIENT
RELATIONSHIPS
IN THE BLINK OF AN EYE

THE
60
SECOND
SALE

DAVID V. LORENZO

WILEY

Published by John Wiley & Sons, Inc., Hoboken, New Jersey.
Published simultaneously in Canada.

For general information on our other products and services or for technical support, please contact our Customer Care Department within the United States at (800) 762-2974, outside the United States at (317) 572-3993, or fax (317) 572-4002.

Wiley publishes in a variety of print and electronic formats and by print-on-demand. Some material included with standard print versions of this book may not be included in e-books or in print-on-demand. If this book refers to media such as a CD or DVD that is not included in the version you purchased, you may download this material at http://booksupport.wiley.com. For more information about Wiley products, visit www.wiley.com.

Library of Congress Cataloging-in-Publication Data

Names: Lorenzo, David V., author.
Title: The 60 second sale : the ultimate system for building lifelong client
    relationships in the blink of an eye / by David V. Lorenzo.
Other titles: Sixty second sale
Description: Hoboken, New Jersey : John Wiley & Sons, Inc., [2018] | Includes
    index. |
Identifiers: LCCN 2018014787 (print) | LCCN 2018015990 (ebook) | ISBN
    9781119499787 (epub) | ISBN 9781119499817 (pdf) | ISBN 9781119499763
    (cloth)
Subjects: LCSH: Selling. | Customer relations. | Sales management.
Classification: LCC HF5438.25 (ebook) | LCC HF5438.25 .L67 2018 (print) | DDC
    658.85—dc23
LC record available at https://lccn.loc.gov/2018014787

Cover Design: Wiley

Printed in the United States of America

10 9 8 7 6 5 4 3 2 1

To Mr. Ralph
You were right.

Contents

How to Use This Book

This book is written as if I am sitting across the table from you, giving you advice. This is the same way I've advised my clients and mentored members of my own sales teams over the years. The guidance dispensed is the same strategy, the same tactics, and the same tools I use each day in my own business. Everything in here works.

If you are skeptical, that's fine. I understand.

Pick out one thing from this program and give it a try. Put it into practice and give it maximum effort. When it works, try something else. Eventually, the system will win you over.

There are two types of people on Planet Earth.

Type 1: People who believe that selling is pushing yourself and your product/service on someone who doesn't need it.

These people hate engaging in the process of selecting a big-ticket item – like buying a car or a diamond ring. They hate it because they fear they will be forced into a bad decision by a fast-talking, slick salesperson.

They can never imagine themselves selling anything to anyone because the concept of asking strangers for money is unbelievably uncomfortable for them. Besides, they hate lying to people and they believe that's the only way to get someone to buy something – by telling the prospective client what they want to hear.

Type 2: People who believe selling is helping people.

These folks develop relationships with everyone. They learn their prospective clients' desires. They learn what their prospective clients want to achieve for their family. They learn what their prospective clients hate and what they fear.

Type 2 people focus on relationships. When you have a relationship with someone and they need help, you feel compelled to help them.

I have three objectives for this book:

1. To give you a step-by-step guide you can follow to open doors, deepen relationships, and make more money.
2. To help get you home on time for dinner every night. I want you to make a great living and live a great life®. This system will help you use the awesome power of leverage to open doors and deepen relationships. That means you don't have to be personally involved in every little detail.
3. To convert as many people as possible from Type 1 to Type 2. It is more personally rewarding to take a relationship-based approach toward sales. Helping people feels good. Helping people in exchange for financial compensation feels good and helps you enjoy life.

Why 60 Seconds?

This book helps you create the atmosphere that allows you to close deals in 60 seconds.

Many people, upon hearing the title of this book, remark that they've never sold anything in 60 seconds. People who say that are wrong. When you have a relationship with someone, a relationship based on trust, people buy from you in 60 seconds. You'll recognize this as you work through this system.

But wait, there's more …

I've included scripts to help you along the way. One of those scripts will help you start a conversation that will lead to a relationship in 60 seconds.

I've also provided email and letter templates to help you engage people, so they will reach out to you and ask you to do business with them. Using these templates and sending them out takes 60 seconds.

Also included is a 21-question interview to help you get inside the mind of your ideal client. It will help you find out what they read, what groups they belong to, and why they do what they do. If you want to meet them and sell to them, you can go where they go, write what they read, and enable them to do what they do. If you do those things, they will buy from you in 60 seconds.

But wait, there's still more …

You will be introduced to a system that drives clients to you while you sleep. That doesn't even take 60 seconds – it takes none of your time!

You will discover my proprietary tool for converting every speaking engagement, article, and advertisement into leads. Deploying that tool takes only 60 seconds.

You will also uncover one change that will stop people cold from saying no to you and get them to say yes. That change takes only 60 seconds to implement.

But wait, here's the most important thing....

Each chapter has actions you should take immediately upon its completion. Chapter 14, "The End of the Beginning," is a guide to making more money based on the principles included in this book. Follow this guide and you will get off to a fast start implementing the information you've discovered. I've even included a video course that corresponds to the book. Visit: http://DoThisSellMore.com to enroll for FREE.

What Now?

The first time you go through this book, read it from beginning to end. Pick out one thing and give it a try.

The second time, go through the book and take the recommended actions at the end of each chapter. Be methodical.

Afterward, use this book as a guide to keep you on track throughout your sales career. It is both a reference and an operations manual. They can drop you into any city, no money in your pocket, with just this book and the clothes on your back, and in 24 hours you'll sell enough to put a roof over your head and food in your belly.

25 Actionable Items from The 60 Second Sale

Below is a quick reference guide to the actionable information contained in these pages. You will use this information throughout your career to open doors, deepen relationships, and make more money.

1. Three guidelines for connecting with people in 60 seconds – **Chapter 1**
2. Script for starting a relationship-based sales conversation – **Chapter 2**
3. Relationship Report Card™: A forecasting tool to predict your financial future – **Chapter 2**
4. Memory jogger with seven categories of people who can expand your natural network – **Chapter 2**
5. Email, direct mail, telephone, and voice mail scripts to initiate contact with people with whom you've lost touch – **Chapter 3**
6. Template for content calendar to be used for email and print newsletters as well as website content – **Chapter 3**
7. Interview questions to help you identify your ideal client, ideal message, and the ideal way to deliver that message – **Chapter 4**
8. Seven-step guide to creating an engagement device called a "honeypot" designed to get people to reach out to you to start a relationship – **Chapter 5**
9. Eleven-step process for attracting new clients through public speaking – **Chapter 6**
10. Five-step guide to creating articles that will help you connect with new clients through publishing – **Chapter 7**
11. Four types of content you must have on your website and how to use them – **Chapter 8**
12. Five formulas for great advertising headlines and great email subject lines – **Chapter 10**
13. Six steps for writing an advertisement that motivates people to call you – **Chapter 10**
14. Five types of testimonials and how to get them from your clients every time you ask – **Chapter 10**
15. Script for starting a conversation at a networking event – **Chapter 11**

16. Five-step process for follow-up after an introduction at a networking event – **Chapter 11**

17. Script for an email introduction between two of your contacts – **Chapter 11**

18. Guide to selecting appropriate networking groups – **Chapter 11**

19. Five steps to making networking groups more productive – **Chapter 11**

20. The step-by-step process for qualifying new clients and making sure they can pay – **Chapter 12**

21. The qualifying script that will change your business forever – **Chapter 12**

22. The five things that you must include in an orientation packet to pre-sell your client – **Chapter 12**

23. Three ways to communicate the value you provide to your client – **Chapter 13**

24. Two sample proposal templates offering options to ensure you get a "yes" every time – **Chapter 13**

25. A checklist for starting an action-oriented sales program today – **Chapter 14**

If you have any questions or you need help, reach out to me:

Website:	DaveLorenzo.com
YouTube:	YouTube.com/DaveLorenzo
Facebook:	@TheDaveLorenzo
Twitter:	@TheDaveLorenzo
Instagram:	@TheDaveLorenzo
Phone:	888.444.5150

If you'd like to put your business growth on the fast track, here are some ways I can help:

Sales Team Training: I develop customized programs for sales teams of all sizes. Together we assess your team's strengths and employ a blend of technology and hands-on instruction to enable sustainable, organic growth.

One-on-one Executive Coaching: Business leaders turn to me for strategic guidance on revenue growth or entering a new market. We also discuss other leadership challenges such as managing a team of high-performing professionals, building strategic alliance partnerships, and other issues that require confidential guidance.

Dave Lorenzo's Strategic Sales Academy: This is my exclusive program for entrepreneurs and sales professionals from all over the world. In this comprehensive session we cover both strategy and tactics that will help you open doors, deepen relationships, and make more money.

Information about these opportunities is available at: Dave Lorenzo.com or by calling 888.444.5150

Introduction: Who Is This Guy?
Why Should I Read This Book?

Cold calling and pushing your way into an office or a living room creates an atmosphere of adversity and distrust you must overcome before you close the deal. With those tired tactics, you're swimming upstream, against a strong current, with a bag of rocks tied to your waist.

Sales has changed.

Legacy sales gimmicks destroy relationships right from the first minute.

This book offers you a turnkey system for building profitable, lifelong relationships. Whether you work with affluent consumers or sell to senior executives in FORTUNE 500 companies, this step-by-step guide will help you open doors, close deals, and make more money in a way that leverages your natural strengths. That's the magnificence of the 60 Second Sale system. You get to be yourself and build your business.

The relationships you develop using the system outlined in this book create the atmosphere that allows you to sell in 60 seconds.

When I take the stage to speak to an enthusiastic audience of business executives, or when I walk into a room to train 50 high-achieving sales professionals, or when I enter a boardroom to meet with a CEO and the company's leadership team, two questions go through the mind of each person staring at me:

- ◆ Who is this guy?
- ◆ Why should I listen to him?

I've got 60 seconds to answer that question or I'm done.

My name is Dave Lorenzo, and the information I'm going to share with you is going to help you make more money and get home, on time, for dinner every night.

If you like money, and you like having control of your life, invest a couple of additional minutes reading this introduction.

How This Whole Thing Got Started

In 2003, I was a partner at The Gallup Organization, an international management consulting company. One day, my boss walked into my office, sat down in the chair across from me, and said, "Dave, listen. I have something I want you to do, and it's something really personal to me."

I sat up, leaned forward, and listened intently as he described a situation in which his ex-brother-in-law, the guy who had divorced his sister, had stolen one of his most prized accounts, a national clothing retailer. He described the pain he felt when his brother-in-law not only humiliated his sister by divorcing her but also stole his account.

He said, "I need you to do me this favor. I need you to drop what you're doing and go after this account as hard as you possibly can. I want you to land this account, and if you do it in the next 60 days, I'm going to give you a $50,000 bonus."

You and I both know that money is a huge motivator for successful sales people, so I sat up in my chair and said, "Boss, you can count on me. I'm on it."

Keep in mind, this was a massive industry. Big ticket, business-to-business consulting is uber-competitive and normally, each deal requires an 18-month (or longer) sales cycle. The minimum size account our company would even consider had to be worth at least $1 million in revenue to us on an annual basis.

I just promised my boss I was going to do this in 60 days.

I slowly looked around the room and I said to myself, "How am I going to make this happen?"

I went into my computer and looked through my contacts file. I searched for people who had been to my speaking engagements who might be able to connect me with someone at the target company. I saw there was one person from this company who had seen me speak and subscribed to our email newsletter. I picked up the phone, gave her a call, and set an appointment to meet her.

At that meeting, I used the techniques we discuss in this book. I created a personal connection with her: I took an interest in her career – in the success she personally desired. In the weeks that followed, I made a genuine effort to help her become successful and, in doing so, closed a deal that produced over $5 million in annual revenue for my company, successfully wrestling the business away from our rival.

The best part?

Because of the trust she developed in me, we cut through all the bureaucracy and reduced an 18-month sales cycle down to close the deal in 60 days. Through this whole process, nothing was more important than the first 60 seconds. The bond between us occurred in that first minute when I demonstrated an external orientation and offered to help her become personally successful.

The 60 Second Sale is all about creating a lifelong bond with your clients – a bond that allows you to become successful by enabling their success.

Selling Is Helping, and I Love to Help People

My career has taken a lot of twists and turns. I started working at the absolute bottom. I was a dishwasher out of high school at a small Italian restaurant and then I became the guy that made the salads. I thought this was my calling, so I went to culinary school. That was an absolute disaster – I hated it.

So, I switched gears and I went to college to pursue a degree in hospitality business and administration while working as a bellhop at Marriott. I worked my way up to manager and eventually managed the Marriott ExecuStay team in New York when it started. In just three years, we went from nothing to $50 million in revenue. After 12 years there and the 9/11 devastation that led to loss of colleagues and clients, it was time move on. I went back to school and got a couple of master's degrees – an MBA from Pace University and a master's degree in strategic communications from Columbia University in New York City.

I was recruited by The Gallup Organization to head up its newly formed Manhattan consulting team. Well, at the time, the team was just me. I worked there for six years, and during my tenure, I developed relationships that produced hundreds of millions in revenue, closed the two largest single consulting contracts in the company's history, and helped keep a huge team of consultants, researchers, and administrative people gainfully employed. My team went from just me with zero revenue to a massive consulting portfolio, generating enormous value for our Fortune 500 clients. I was successful in all the standard ways. And then everything changed...

The Wake-Up Call

Are you in control of your business, your career, and your future?

One cold winter morning, I was not focused on the answer to that question. I was not focused on anything. I was flat on my back, strapped to a wooden board on a gurney. I stared at the ceiling, counting the tiles that passed by as the paramedics and doctors pushed me faster and faster down a seemingly endless hallway. Everything below my shoulders was numb. My mind was making up for the lack of motion in my body. It was racing with blistering speed. I was not thinking about the things I would not be able to do if the feeling did not return. I was thinking about my priorities. I was thinking specifically about all the family things, all the life things I had put off because I thought my work and my life could not coexist.

It is amazing how your life can change in a split second.

Earlier that morning, I was at my office at Gallup and I made a choice to drop off a file at a client's office instead of meeting my wife for lunch. I could have sent a messenger with the file. I could have emailed the documents. I could have done several different things, but the client demanded I bring the file personally so he could review the work and give me immediate feedback.

I walked at a brisk pace as I stepped off the curb with the rest of the pedestrians crossing with the light, in the crosswalk. I was not on my mobile phone. I was not distracted. I was thinking about crossing the street.

When the Yellow Cab hit me, time stood still. I could see the horror on the faces of the other pedestrians as I flew 24 feet, 7 inches and hit the ground with a sickening thud. I remember hearing the commotion as a group of good Samaritans chased down the cab driver and pulled him out of the cab. I also remember the kind woman who asked me if she could call someone as they loaded me into the ambulance.

Back in the hospital, my focus changed when the ceiling tiles gave way to a long metal tube into which I was carefully loaded by four hospital staffers. The only thing louder than the annoying hum of the equipment was the sound of my thoughts. Thoughts of things I had yet to do. Things I had put off. Quality time I had not spent with people in my life who really mattered.

Don't worry – things worked out for me after that day … in more ways than one.

By the grace of God, I suffered no lasting injuries from that accident, but it served as a wake-up call. I made the decision that from that day forward, my work was going to be something that enabled my life. I was going to be passionate about every aspect of my work and I was going to delegate things I did not enjoy. I was only going to accept clients who energized me, and I was not going to let anyone dictate the terms under which I would operate. I would take time to do things that were important both for my clients and my family. And I would make those two previously competing forces live in harmony in my life.

Over a decade later, life is still a work in progress, but it is a process I am enjoying, each and every single day.

Not long after that accident, I went out on my own. Again, I started from scratch. I had no accounts. No prospects – my non-compete agreement prohibited me from even talking to clients and prospects I had worked with or called on while at Gallup. The only thing I had was a burning desire to help people take control of their future through relationship-based sales, something that I was innately good at.

These days, I define success a little differently. Success to me today isn't only about the biggest client I can get or the biggest sale I can make. It's about doing those things on my own terms. It's about controlling my own destiny and my own time – what I want to do, when I want to do it.

That's the value I provide. That's what this system does. It helps people make lots of money without compromising their beliefs. It helps people take control of their lives.

Ask yourself these three questions:

1. Are you delivering maximum value to each of your clients?
2. Are you proud of the impact you have on others each day while you are at work?
3. Are you in control of your business, your career, and your future?

If you answered no to any of those questions, this is the most important book you'll read this year.

I was able to answer yes to those first two questions but not to the third. It took getting run down by a taxicab for me to realize how important the answer to that question really is.

Your life can change in 60 seconds.

Just as importantly, you can help change the life of someone else in 60 seconds. Make them matter. My mission is to enable sales executives, business leaders, and independent professionals in all industries make a great living and live a great life.

My 60 Second Sale process makes each minute a profit opportunity for you.

In the pages that follow, I will lay out an entire system for you and give you the step-by-step activities to help you open doors, deepen relationships, and make more money.

Here is a sneak peek at what you are about to discover:

◆ How to start a sales conversation in 60 seconds
◆ Who to target for immediate income
◆ A powerful yet easy-to-use system to generate relationship revenue
◆ Five ways to initiate new relationships
◆ What to say to make sure your business meetings result in money in the bank
◆ The secret to getting a "yes" every time, even in the most competitive sales environment
◆ The winning mind-set that removes the stress, uncertainty, and fear from income generation
◆ And so many other effective business growth strategies, your competition won't know what hit them

THE
60
SECOND
SALE

Chapter 1

It Was Never about the Pen

60 Second Summary

Sales has changed.

Once upon a time, you walked into an office and knocked on a door and offered something to potential buyers. If they said they wanted what you had to offer, you negotiated a price. Once they paid, you moved on to the next office or knocked on the next door.

Sales is no longer transactional. It's now about relationships. You can't even get to the door upon which to knock without a relationship. You can't get into the office without a relationship.

If you want to sell now, you must start by selling yourself and selling your interest in helping the prospective client succeed.

What's in This Chapter for You?

This chapter will help change your thinking about sales and selling. You will begin to focus on relationships not transactions. When you do, you'll be in the minority: people leading a relationship-based business today. This gives you an advantage.

Imagine that.

Your competitive advantage is the way you look at the world of business and the way you approach each person with whom you come into contact.

In 60 seconds, you'll open doors, deepen relationships, and make more money because you think differently.

The key concept you will discover in this chapter is called *external orientation*. That means focusing on meeting the needs of the other person before asking them to take action on your behalf. Understand them and seek to help them achieve a goal or relieve some pain before you sell to them.

This type of thinking is the ultimate competitive advantage.

The Dumbest Sales Interview Question in History

"Can you sell me this pen?"

One of the dumbest things I've seen is a sales executive, in an interview, use this hackneyed question to determine if someone is qualified as a sales professional.

You see it in the movies. You see it on talk shows. It's used everyday in sales interviews. The idea behind the question is, if you can sell the pen to the person sitting across the desk, under pressure, you can sell anything to anyone.

The problem: Before you get to have a conversation about the pen, you need to know the answers to a whole host of other questions, like:

Why is this person buying pens?

Does the person's success in a pen purchase advance his or her career?

What can you do, beyond providing this pen, to advance that person's career? How can you help the pen buyer succeed?

So what do you do? What's the correct answer?

The correct answer is to say: "Mr. Buyer, I want to help you with more than just the pen. I'm in this for the long term. Take the pen and use it for as long as you'd like. Now tell me a little about what you do here and how your success is measured."

You're not in the business of giving away things you'd normally be able to make money selling, but if forced into a situation that makes you choose between a transaction and a relationship, you should choose the relationship every time.

Selling a pen to someone on the spot is a transaction. Helping the guy who buys the pens grow his business and advance his career is developing a relationship.

Office Supplies by Referral Only

Can you imagine a waiting list to have lunch with an office supply salesperson? Well, it actually happened to a man named Ralph Liparulo. "Mr. Ralph," as he was known, spent the last decade of his 56-year career selling office supplies. He wasn't focused on selling pens. He was focused on helping people make money.

How can the guy who sells office supplies become the person who influences careers?

Mr. Ralph was in and out of offices all day long. While he stopped in an office, he talked with the business owner or manager about what they did, who their clients were, and the value they provided.

One day, he stopped by a customer's office and found it was flooded. The carpet was soaked. Mr. Ralph jumped on the phone and called a carpet cleaning company, who also happened to be his customer. The timing was excellent, and they had water extractors on the scene within the hour. Both the carpet company and the customer with the flood were thrilled.

This gave Mr. Ralph an idea. Each week, he began dedicating two hours to calling existing clients and referring them to each other. He'd schedule one breakfast and one lunch each week to introduce his customers to each other. He wouldn't sell any office products at these meetings. He'd simply introduce the two people and talk about what they did and the value they provided.

His clients viewed Mr. Ralph as someone who took a genuine interest in them and the growth of their business. He wasn't the guy selling pens. He was way more valuable than that.

Over time, Mr. Ralph was able to stop cold calling. He lived off the referrals these clients passed him. His weekly introduction meals became almost a daily routine. His clients not only rewarded him with more frequent orders, they also introduced him to their colleagues.

Office supplies were a commodity, but a relationship with Mr. Ralph was a unique opportunity to grow your business with every order of pens, copy paper, and legal pads. People would buy office supplies just to be introduced to Mr. Ralph's network.

External Orientation: Relationships, Not Transactions

What did Mr. Ralph discover that his competition, and almost every sales professional in the world, missed? He unlocked the awesome power of relationship-based sales.

Everyone else in his industry was knocking on doors trying to sell pens. Mr. Ralph was trying to help people achieve their goals. He had what I call an *external orientation*. This means he placed the benefit of the other person ahead of his need to achieve his goal.

If you want to connect with people in 60 seconds, you have to show them you can help them achieve a goal or solve a problem.

Here are three guidelines to keep you focused:

1. For every conversation, 70% should be focused on the other person. Stop talking. People do not care about you until they believe you have their best interests in mind. This means you have to shut up and let them do the talking.
2. When people talk to you, they tell you their problems and their goals. People want help but they don't want to ask for help. Sometimes they are too embarrassed to ask. Sometimes their pride gets in the way of asking. But if you allow people to open up, they will tell you what they truly desire. That will give you the opportunity to help.
3. When you solve problems, you make money. Most sales professionals look for problems their product can solve. When that particular problem hits them in the face, they are great at matching the benefits of their product to the needs expressed by the customer. Where they fall short is when the customer expresses a problem outside the scope of their normal work. Usually, the salesperson will run away as fast as possible. But that is a true opportunity to build a relationship.

Somebody Call Security

There are so many preconceived ideas about how sales is supposed to be done, we all fall victim to some bad habits that are thought of as accepted sales practices.

I made this mistake when I first began my career as a consultant. Based in New York, I flew to Boston for three meetings with prospective clients. The three meetings were set by a team member, and the first two went well. At the first meeting with a large regional bank, I showed up, asked questions, and offered thoughts on how we could provide value. The second meeting was a follow-up meeting, and I shared some information on a solution we previously presented.

After lunch, I was scheduled to go to the third meeting. While preparing for the meeting, I was told the CEO of this men's plus-size clothing brand wanted a presentation of my company's capabilities, so I dragged a projector and a computer along with me on this trip, and to the previous meetings, so I could do the full dog-and-pony show.

I arrived 30 minutes early for the meeting. I set up the projector and computer and tested everything.

When the executive and his entourage arrived, I introduced myself to all of them and immediately began my presentation. About three slides into the show, the CEO interrupted me and said, "Dave, just tell us what you think you can do for our company."

I smiled and said I was about to get to that part of the presentation.

And I pressed on.

I continued to talk about our offices in 14 different countries and our vast research capabilities – never once asking about the CEO's issues or the challenges facing the company with whom I was meeting.

The CEO stopped me again:

"Can you just get to the part where you tell us how you can help us?" he reiterated.

I nodded and moved on to the next slide and before I got halfway through the points related to it, I noticed the CEO get up and pick up a telephone in the corner of the room.

About three minutes later, two large men in suits appeared in the doorway and escorted me out of the room. They waited with me in the lobby as an assistant packed up my projector and computer and brought them to me.

I had been physically thrown out of the meeting for not building a relationship.

On the plane home that evening I reflected upon my day. I thought about what went well in the first two meetings and what went horribly wrong in the third. When I got to the office, I put the projector away and never brought it to a "sales meeting" again.

I don't do sales meetings anymore. Sure, I still sell things. In fact, I sell something (or at least try to) every day. But the meetings I host and attend now are called business meetings because we discuss how we can work together and exchange value. My client needs help solving a problem or achieving a goal, and I receive financial compensation for helping achieve those outcomes.

That's business.

That's the tectonic mind-set shift you need to make if you want to take greater control of your business, your income, and your life. "Selling" is helping. When you "sell," you exchange value for compensation. If your prospective clients like you and trust you, they will invest in you.

My way of "selling" is by developing a relationship with clients, listening to them, and then helping them solve their problems. The key is to put the relationship ahead of any transaction.

That's your job in the first 60 seconds – sell the prospective client on a relationship with you.

Within the first minute of your interaction with any prospective clients, they are deciding if you care about them and their business or if you only care about closing the deal. If they sense any doubt about whether you have an external orientation, you will not be able to recover.

You've probably heard the phrase, "You never get a second chance to make a first impression." Well, in business, if you don't demonstrate your external orientation within the first 60 seconds, you'll never have another chance with that prospective client.

People often tell me relationships are nice but they take time to develop. They say they need to make money today. They've got bills to pay and they can't wait to develop relationships with people who probably need what they are selling right now.

First: Those people are wrong. Relationships can be initiated, developed, and consummated quickly – like love at first sight.

Second: You already have relationships that you can count on to deliver business to your doorstep. You just have not cultivated them properly.

Third: The people who say this are focused on transactions. They practice what I call "hit-and-run" sales. They want to shake your hand when they meet you, spew some information about their product or service, take the money, and shake your hand as they leave the room. Then they move on to the next transaction.

Times have changed, and sales has changed. The hit-and-run sales approach doesn't work anymore. We are in a time when everything from shoes to airplanes can be researched and purchased without any human interaction. This means the *experience* of working with someone who can solve your problem must be outstanding. This experience starts with a relationship.

Why Relationship–Based Sales? Five Reasons

In case you need more convincing, let me appeal to your self-interest and give you five reasons why relationships are better than transactions.

MONEY ON DEMAND

When you focus on establishing and cultivating relationships, you have a limitless source of income. You can pick up the phone and have a conversation with a current client, former client, prospective client, or someone who refers you business, and any one of them can deliver some new revenue to you immediately. That is the pure 60 Second Sale.

CONFIDENCE

As a respected confidant – someone who is valuable and delivers valuable solutions to people – you are welcomed into offices, high-level meetings, and confidential conversations. This boosts your self-esteem. The key to success in offering solutions is having the courage to pick up the phone and reach out to people. People with high self-esteem have no problem doing that.

In short, you feel better about yourself, and when you do, you reach out aggressively to help people. When you help people, you feel better. It is a cycle.

PRIDE

You're delivering value for people – everyone with whom you interact. You're connecting people with others who can help them, or you're solving problems for them yourself. That is a noble calling. Once you have success with this system, you'll want to do it all the time. It's addicting.

Painless Process Management

Sales professionals and business leaders are obsessed with their *pipeline*. Their future success is supposedly based on:

- How many new appointments they have
- How many meetings they have attended
- How many proposals they've written
- How many deals they've closed
- How many of their clients have paid

This is a typical approach to sales management. It is administratively onerous. It requires teams of people working behind the scenes just to keep track of the activity and reporting compliance. It creates layers of bureaucracy involved in supporting the sales organization.

With relationship-based sales, you keep track of each relationship and make a few notes about the last conversation you've had and the goals, plans, and desires of your clients and referral sources.

There is no need for layers upon layers of management. There is no need for bureaucracy. There's also no need for endless, tedious meetings that keep sales professionals from doing what they should be doing – talking to clients.

Relationship Income

A few times each month, people who know you, like you, and trust you will call and ask you for help.

You won't see these calls coming. They'll come when you don't expect them, but you will immediately recognize the name of the person reaching out to you. Maybe you helped someone with something small, years ago, or maybe you referred business to the person without even giving it a second thought.

That's passive income, and it arrives because of your focus on developing relationships.

Four Types of Income

In sales, there are four potential types of revenue (Figure 1.1).

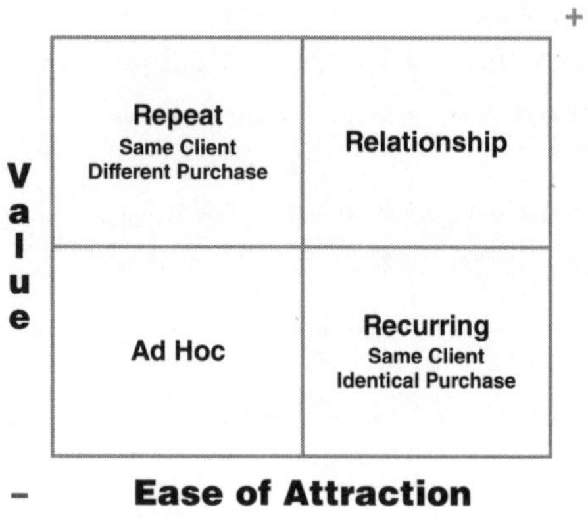

FIGURE **1.1**   Four Types of Income

AD HOC

This is transactional revenue. It is what the typical sales professional focuses on, and it is what 90% of the sales universe is chasing right now.

This type of income requires only enough trust to close the initial deal. If you are selling pens to businesses, it only requires enough trust that you will deliver pens that write, on time, and in the right color.

Attracting this type of revenue is tough. You have to go out and knock on doors over and over again. You bang your head against the wall 10 times to get one yes.

REPEAT REVENUE

This is revenue developed from contacts you initiate. You realize it from the sale of a product or service the client has not previously purchased from you.

You call the client and introduce him to a product or service he hasn't used from your company. This requires a high level of trust, because the client has not used your firm for this service in the past. It is not as difficult to generate as ad hoc revenue because the client already knows you, likes you, and trusts you – but the client doesn't trust your ability to deliver this particular product or service. That is still yet to be earned.

Revenue from cross-selling is considered repeat revenue.

Note: If you are in a business where the repeat revenue must come from another service center, you risk losing control of the client relationship. That's why trust is paramount in the repeat revenue sector.

RECURRING REVENUE

This is revenue from the same activity done over and over again.

For example: You sign a contract with the federal government to provide desk chairs. Every time someone in the government needs a desk chair, you get the call. All day long you take orders for desk chairs and only desk chairs.

Here's a second example: You are a printer and you have a contract to provide printing to franchisees of a pack and mail company. You've negotiated a special price for three different documents each franchisee needs. A different company calls each day, but it is for the same printing package.

This revenue can come from the same client, as in the federal government example, or different clients, as in the example of the franchisee.

Recurring revenue is valuable to you because it is more predictable than ad hoc revenue. Recurring revenue doesn't need a high level of trust on the part of the client because you've proven your ability to deliver over and over again. There is little risk on the part of the client.

RELATIONSHIP REVENUE

The client calls you, unsolicited, for help or advice. These clients call because they trust you and know you have their best interest at heart.

My distinction of repeat revenue from relationship revenue is that repeat revenue is initiated by you and relationship revenue is initiated by the client.

There is another form of relationship revenue – referrals.

You can source referrals from clients who have used your services and you can receive referrals from people who trust you but have never used your services. We call the later *evangelists*.

Relationship revenue is the Holy Grail of sales income because it flows to you with no additional effort on your part. It is truly passive income that arrives on your doorstep while you sleep, go sailing, play golf, or take your family on vacation.

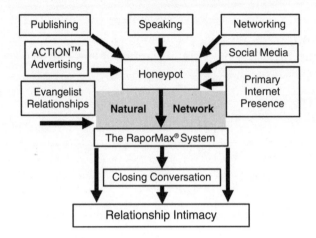

Figure 1.2   The 60 Second Sale System

You Need a System

If you want relationship income to show up on your doorstep, you need to make sure you cultivate relationships. This is tough to do while you are developing new relationships, doing work, and living your life.

That's why you need a system.

Your system must keep track of the new people with whom you connect. The system must keep track of people who refer you business. It must keep track of everything you do with your clients. And it must cultivate relationships with all of those constituencies with frequency (Figure 1.2).

If you tried to do this on your own, with no plan, no goal, and no system, you'd have a nervous breakdown ... or you'd only be able to focus on one thing at a time.

60 Second Actions

◆ Now that you've finished this chapter, take one minute and think about the business you developed in the past six months. Write down how much revenue came from each of the four sources.
   • How much was ad hoc?
   • How much was recurring?

- How much was repeat?
- How much was relationship?

◆ Write down the names of the clients who provided you with relationship revenue. Make a quick bullet-point list of everything you know about them and their businesses.

◆ Spend some time looking through your contacts. Is there someone you can introduce each of those relationship revenue clients to in order to improve their businesses or help them achieve their goals. (If you don't know the goals of these clients, get on the phone and start some conversations.)

◆ Make at least one introduction in the next 24 hours.

Chapter 2

The First 60 Seconds Sets the Tone for a Lifetime

60 Second Summary

This chapter will help you start new business relationships in the most productive way possible. That not only means more money in your pocket now, it also means more money over the lifetime of your relationship with the client.

The Relationship Report Card™ score is a leading indicator for your success as a sales professional. Take the assessment and determine your rank.

If you are a business leader, you can use the Relationship Report Card™ to measure the success of sales professionals on your team. The higher the score, the deeper the relationships and the more money driven into the organization.

What's in This Chapter for You?

After implementing the concepts in this chapter, you can expect to open new doors to productive, profitable relationships. You will also improve your focus on the day-to-day activities that drive relationship growth.

This focus on deepening relationships will be the foundation upon which you will build your new sales system – one which will create an atmosphere where it is possible to make sales in 60 seconds.

The key concept you will discover in this chapter is the Relationship Report Card™. This 10-question assessment will help you evaluate the strength of your relationship development skills and forecast your ability to establish and grow business relationships.

The Old Way: Show Up and Throw Up

You stand in the doorway of a hotel meeting room. The familiar smell of mildew in the air-conditioning vents, stale coffee, and prepackaged breakfast pastry hits you right in the face.

You take two steps into the room and, out of thin air, a short man in a white shirt, checkered tie, and black slacks stops you. He's been eating an onion bagel with lox and capers. (You smell it on his breath – he's that close.) He thrusts a business card into your hand and says:

> "I'm Neil Sims and here's a quick computer tip for you. To close your windows in Microsoft® office hit the control key and the letter W. Would you like to take a training course with me to get more great tips like these?"

Suddenly, you vomit a little into your mouth, and, like a confused passenger in an airplane that has just crashed, you forget that the nearest exit is behind you. You're looking for a way out, and when you fix your gaze back on Neil, you realize he's still talking as his breath turns up the corners of the stick-on name tag you have on your lapel.

This is an awkward moment.

Unfortunately, it also happens to be a true story. It happened to me at a chamber of commerce business networker when I started my consulting company.

This is the standard approach employed by most folks who are trying to sell something. It's in your face and it forces information on you like water from a firehose.

There is a better way to invest those critical 60 seconds when you first meet someone.

Clarity of Purpose: Start a Relationship

Your approach to starting a sales conversation will forecast your intention for the future of the relationship. If you knock on a door to a home and immediately offer your goods to the person who answers, your intention is solely to make money.

If you reach out to people you suspect may need your service (and not everyone indiscriminately), ask them about their goals, and offer to help them achieve those goals, regardless of your potential financial gain, it becomes clear your purpose is to initiate a relationship.

How to Start a Sales Conversation in 60 Seconds

As we walk to the car, Kary, my wife, says, "Make sure you're ready to talk about what you do. There are going to be a lot of senior executives at this party, and this is the perfect place for you to tell them how you can help them."

We are going to a birthday party for a friend who has worked for three companies in the Fortune 500.

I'm nauseous during the entire 20-minute trip.

I am much more comfortable on a stage, speaking to an audience of 1,000 people, than I am at a cocktail party standing face-to-face, belly-to-belly, with someone I don't know.

Nevertheless, I realized early on in my career as a business owner (and as a husband) that I couldn't go through life only speaking with buffet attendants and bartenders at social functions. I knew if I got the other person talking, and kept them talking, I could relax.

I decided to approach this situation like a researcher. I created and tested different "scripts" for conversations and eventually settled on a dialogue that was most effective. As soon as I began asking people about themselves, what they did for a living, and their ambition, people began to open up to me in ways I never imagined (even without plying them with alcohol).

As it turns out, people like talking about themselves so much, this became a great way to start sales conversations. Now I use the "script" everywhere. This past summer I used it to get an appointment with a business owner while waiting in line for a ride at a theme park.

As you read through it, keep in mind the exact wording of each question is not as important as the thought process. When you start a conversation using these questions, in this way, you are doing three important things:

1. You are breaking the ice and getting the person in front of you to feel comfortable and start talking.
2. You're showing them you are focused on them. You're not selfish. You're intellectually curious.

3. After demonstrating a substantial amount of goodwill, you offer assistance in helping them achieve a goal or solve a problem.

OPENING QUESTION

The objective of the opening question and follow-up is to make those you are talking to feel comfortable and get them talking about themselves.

◆ What do you do for work (for a living)?

Follow-up

◆ How did you get into that?

The follow-up question is important because it shows you're interested in the other person. It shows you want to learn more. It helps others open up and share their lives with you.

QUESTION 1: HOW'S LIFE?

Next, we ask about the current economic state or their business. This question is designed to be asked innocently, as if you are two friends talking. If the person is not in business and you are not in business-to-business sales, substitute the word "life" for "business."

◆ How is business (life)?

Follow-up

◆ What goals do you have for the next (month, year)? Or
◆ What are you working on right now? Or
◆ What are you most concerned about?

QUESTION 2: WHAT'S IT MEAN TO YOU?

This question is the most important part of this sequence. It takes the goals and makes them personal. In our approach to sales, we sell to people, even in a business-to-business. Remember, we work with and help *people*. That's why we need to know how achieving the goals will have a personal impact on the prospective client.

◆ How will achieving that help you personally? Or
◆ Why is that so important to you? Or
◆ What will that mean for your life?

QUESTION 3: WHAT'S STOPPING YOU?

Now your prospective client is talking and feeling good about the conversation they are having with you. At this point, you can ask about any barriers that are in the way. The questions should flow in a conversational format.

- What is keeping you from achieving your goals? Or
- What is keeping that from happening? Or
- What's holding you back?

QUESTION 4: HOW CAN I HELP?

The final question is about you helping remove any barriers keeping the client from achieving a goal. During the course of this conversation, you might have identified an opportunity to directly help. At that point, you ask if the person wants assistance.

If you cannot directly help, you can make a referral to someone who can. In that case, you'd ask who you can connect the person to for assistance.

- Would you like some help with that? Or
- Who can I connect you with to help you?

Beginning a relationship with this type of conversation demonstrates your external orientation and lends itself to two possible immediately identifiable outcomes:

- *Possible new client relationship:* The person with whom you are speaking raises an immediate issue and you are qualified to help resolve it. In this case, you can schedule a business meeting to discuss the issue in detail. In this scenario, this person is a prospective client.
- *Possible referral relationship:* The person with whom you are speaking raises an issue and you are unable to directly help. Listen to the issue carefully and search your memory to uncover anyone you may know who can help. Often, if you ask a few follow-up questions, you will realize you know someone to whom you can refer this person.

This specific scenario highlights the importance of building a strong, diverse network of resources. Your mission is to become "the person to call when they don't know who to call."

Five Million Reasons to Be a Resource

A few months after the birth of my son, I decided to get serious about my finances. I met with several financial advisors and didn't get a warm and fuzzy feeling from any of them. Some had clinical approaches to portfolio management. Some used formulas. Some relied on institutional depth of knowledge.

There was nobody focused on me and my future. Everyone was focused on the money.

After a while, I started thinking that money was so central to the role of a financial advisor, it would be difficult to find someone with a strong relationship focus. I wished I could help convert some of the folks in this role to my point of view about sales and selling. I decided to withhold my proselytizing to this group of people until after I produced a fantastic sales book they could read and absorb.

So, I sat on my money and postponed that decision.

Around the same time, I met a gentleman named Perry Greenfield. Perry and I belonged to a business group, and we had breakfast together each week. Within a few weeks of meeting him, Perry began introducing me to people he thought would help my business grow. Being a native of south Florida, Perry also helped my family integrate into the community through social activities.

In short, Perry put the relationship first.

After a few years, it was an easy decision to work with him as my financial advisor.

Two years ago, I attended a holiday party at the home of a friend. While enjoying some hor d'oeuvres and holiday cheer, I struck up a conversation with one of the other attendees. I used the script as outlined above. Here's how the conversation went:

"Hello my name is Dave. What's your name?"

"My name is Linda," the woman answered. (Note: I changed the woman's name to protect her confidentiality.)

"It's nice to meet you, Linda. How do you know our hosts?" I replied.

"I'm their neighbor and we met while walking our dogs," Linda said.

"Tell me, Linda, what do you do for a living?" I asked.

"I sell medical supplies, but I spend a lot of my time taking care of my sister. She was injured in an accident a number of years ago."

"I'm sorry to hear that. Taking care of her must take up a great deal of time. How do you manage to find time to sell?" I asked.

"Well, actually my sister has round-the-clock help. My role is to take care of all the bills that come along with her care and condition," Linda continued.

"Wow. You must be great at sales! That level of care is expensive," I replied.

"No. No," she laughed. "My sister received a large amount of money in a lawsuit as a result of her accident. I use the money from that to pay the bills."

"That's interesting. What is the biggest challenge with that role – being the administrator of those finances?"

"You know, right now I am really struggling with the people who manage the trust fund. They have not been responsive to me, and they are dismissive of my ideas for investing some of the money. My sister is young and we need to invest wisely and conservatively so the money lasts a long time. I need to make a change. I don't have confidence in these people any longer," Linda said.

"Would you like some help with that?" I asked.

"What do you mean? Do you manage money?" she replied.

"No. But I help many professionals grow their businesses, and I know the perfect person to give you some insight on this situation. He happens to be my financial advisor. I trust him implicitly," I said.

"That would be great. I'd love to meet him," Linda said.

I introduced Linda to Perry. The two of them got along well, and, after Linda met Perry's team, she transferred the entire trust, over $5 million, to Perry for management.

There are three important things to highlight in the application of this script:

1. I adapted the language to fit the conversation. Do not get hung up on the specifics of the verbiage. The idea is to get people to open up and share their problems and goals with you. You want to be of service in some way, but you cannot just walk up to somebody you don't know and ask about their problems. You have to ease into it through appropriate conversation.

2. I had a solution, and I didn't hesitate to share it with Linda immediately. Sometimes you will need to give some thought to helping a person you meet under these conditions. But often, you will know someone right away. When you do, make the offer to help immediately. This shows that you are serious about providing assistance.

3. It may appear as if I have not received any benefit from making this introduction and I've taken a risk. What if Linda becomes dissatisfied with Perry? She might blame me.

That's not the way to view it. Linda is an adult. She can evaluate Perry and his team both now and into the future.

As for the benefit to me: Both of those folks regularly send me referrals. They actively try to help me grow my business. I've got two great advocates out in the world who think about me all the time as a result of this referral.

Every Interaction Is an Opportunity of a Lifetime

The story of Perry and Linda is just one example of the lifetime value potential of a relationship. Think about things from Perry's perspective. I'm his client so he's already happy with the business I've given him but let's say, hypothetically, he makes $2,500 each year from the work we do together. Over the course of 10 years, my business is worth $25,000 to him. But because of the relationship he has with me, I referred him a $5 million trust to manage. If he earns one-half of 1% for managing that money, he will make $25,000 per year from that relationship. Over 10 years, that's $250,000. What if Perry maintains both relationships for 20 years? Even with no additional investment, as long as things remain the same, the value of Perry's relationship with me is worth over $550,000.

I realize there are several assumptions made in that example, but think about the work required on Perry's part to have the opportunity. He didn't need any additional effort, compared to other advisors who practice transactional, hit-and-run sales. He just needed a different approach. Instead of looking at me and my portfolio as an opportunity to just sign-up someone and move on, he invested his time and interest in me.

Perry is always looking to help me grow my business. He is always looking to keep me in the loop on opportunities for my kids to learn and grow.

The difference is in attitude and approach toward the client relationship. The tired advice of "make more calls and make more money" focuses on volume and not on intensity.

Put another way, if you only have 10 relationships and 5 of them are worth an average of $1,000, are you better off than someone with 1,000 relationships worth $5 each? Well, given that each relationship requires the same amount of effort to acquire and maintain, if you have 5 high-value relationships, you can still get home for dinner each night.

Reduction in labor intensity is an underestimated benefit of this approach of relationship-based sales.

How to Track and Forecast Relationship Growth

Now that you know how to start a relationship-based sales conversation in 60 seconds, you need a way to keep track of your efficacy. Money in the bank is a good measurement of success, but how will you know if you are on the right track with your relationships?

Here are the 10 leading indicators of high lifetime value relationships:

◆ A focus on relationship growth
◆ Advisory status

- ◆ Referability
- ◆ Frequency of communication
- ◆ Client testimonials
- ◆ Aggressive promotion in advancement of client interest
- ◆ Commitment to relationship intensity
- ◆ Gratitude
- ◆ Intimacy
- ◆ Passion for service

Your commitment to each of these elements is critical to your success in developing a portfolio with high lifetime value. Let's break down each element and discuss its impact on your ability to open doors, deepen relationships, and make more money.

A Focus on Relationship Growth
This cuts to the heart of your clarity of purpose. Do you enter each interaction looking to begin a relationship or do you enter looking to extract cash, scorch the earth, and move on?

Advisory Status
A client must see you as someone who can look into the future and determine what issues will impact him and his company in the days, weeks, months, and years to come.

Advisors have enormous value. Salespeople are viewed as a means to an end. Be an advisor.

Referability
It must be easy for your clients to connect you with other people. Make it effortless for others to offer a relationship with you as a solution to their problems.

Frequency of Communication
The more often you speak with someone, the deeper your relationship becomes. This is one of the key elements of any relationship. Communication is its lifeblood. When you increase communication frequency, you open doors, deepen relationships, and make more money.

CLIENT TESTIMONIALS

It requires significant effort to say something positive about another person, loudly and proudly. When people give you this kind of praise, it reflects their commitment to you. If you are receiving testimonials, you're clearly helping people. That is a leading indicator of positive relationships.

AGGRESSIVE PROMOTION OF CLIENT INTERESTS

How do you help your client after the sale? Do you promote their business? The fastest way to attract attention and interest from someone is to put money in their pocket. It doesn't matter if you sell pens or tractors, heavy jets or facelifts. Once someone has used your product or service, that's not the end of your relationship – that's the beginning. Your support for a client's business is a leading indicator of how strong your relationship can become.

COMMITMENT TO RELATIONSHIP INTENSITY

I use the baseball test to help me determine how strong my relationship is with my clients. If my client would enjoy sitting next to me at a baseball game for three hours, I'm doing something right. Face-to-face interaction is powerful because it demonstrates commitment to a relationship. There is no substitute for it. If you believe in that concept enough to take time from your schedule to sit and speak with at least one client each month, in person, you're probably going to be great at developing deep relationships.

GRATITUDE

Say, "Thank you." How difficult is that? Focus on appreciation for business and the relationships in your business. This helps reinforce the behavior you want. People will gladly refer you and invest in you because they know how much you appreciate it.

Your aggressive demonstration of gratitude is a leading indicator for strength of relationship.

INTIMACY

If you become part of the fabric of a client's life, it becomes difficult for them to unplug from you. That's why attendance at life events is a leading indicator of strength of client relationships. If you attend weddings, birthdays, retirement parties, and other life events, you are a significant part of your client's life. You've taken your relationship beyond business.

PASSION FOR SERVICE

Your commitment to the products and solutions you provide to your clients is an essential leading indicator for the depth of your relationships. Your commitment to your ability to help is fundamental. Demonstrate zealousness for what you do and you'll have a strong foundation upon which to build your client relationship.

Measurement and Forecasting

Whenever I meet with business leaders, CEOs, entrepreneurs, professionals, and sales managers, they ask me to look into the future and forecast which sales professional will be successful at building and growing their book of business with relationship-based sales. That's why I've developed a self-assessment called the Relationship Report Card™.

There are 10 survey items that measure the intensity of the sales professional's commitment to relationship-based business development:

1. What percentage of your business is relationship revenue?
2. I receive calls each month from clients asking me for advice unrelated to work I am currently doing.
3. I receive at least one referral from a client each month.
4. I keep in touch with my clients.
5. I receive testimonials, letters of recommendation, and notes of thanks from clients.
6. I refer at least one of my clients to people who can invest in their services.
7. I hold a face-to-face meeting with at least one client.
8. I express my gratitude to everyone who has invested in me and my services.
9. I attend life events for clients.
10. I am passionate about my ability to make a difference for my clients.

The sales professional is asked to rate each item honestly. Each answer has a corresponding numeric value. After completing the self-assessment, the individual then tallies the score and measures improvement over time.

Relationship Report Card™

1. **What percentage of your business is relationship revenue?**

   Less than 10% – 0

   Between 11% and 20% – 1

   Between 21% and 50% – 2

   Between 51% and 70% – 3

   Between 71% and 80% – 4

   More than 80% – 5

2. **I receive calls each month from clients asking me for advice unrelated to work I am currently doing.**

   Never – 0

   About 25% of the time – 1

   About half the time – 2

   About 75% of the time – 3

   About 90% of the time – 4

   Every month without fail – 5

3. **I receive at least one referral from a client each month.**

   Never – 0

   About 25% of the time – 1

   About half the time – 2

   About 75% of the time – 3

   About 90% of the time – 4

   Every month without fail – 5

4. **I keep in touch with my clients.**

   Never – 0

   Annually – 1

Twice per year – 2

Quarterly – 3

Monthly – 4

Weekly – 5

5. I receive testimonials, letters of recommendation, and notes of thanks from clients.

Never – 0

Annually – 1

Twice per year – 2

Quarterly – 3

Monthly – 4

Weekly – 5

6. I refer at least one of my clients to people who can invest in their services.

Never – 0

One time each year – 1

Two times each year – 2

Four times each year – 3

Monthly – 4

Weekly – 5

7. I hold a face-to-face meeting with at least one client.

Never – 0

One time each year – 1

Two times each year – 2

Four times each year – 3

Monthly – 4

Weekly – 5

8. I express my gratitude to everyone who has invested in me and my services.

Yes – 5

No – 0

9. I attend life events for clients.

Never – 0

One time each year – 1

Two times each year – 2

Four times each year – 3

Monthly – 4

Weekly – 5

10. I am passionate about my ability to make a difference for my clients.

Not at all – 0

Slightly – 1

As much as the average person in my role – 2

Above average – 3

Wildly passionate – 4

Fanatical; I eat, sleep, and breathe my passion for making a difference for clients. – 5

Measurement of your own performance improvement is critical for success. As a way to help provide additional incentive for relationship development, I've worked with several organizations to create a hierarchy for recognition.

Here is a sample hierarchy based on total score on the Relationship Report Card™:

Clear = New hire or novice; Total Relationship Report Card™ score below 20

Bronze = Relationship Report Card™ score between 21 and 30

Silver = Relationship Report Card™ score between 31 and 40

Gold = Relationship Report Card™ score between 41 and 45

Platinum = Relationship Report Card™ score above 45

Some organizations have adopted this scoring system for their performance appraisal process. In that case, the sales professional is asked to provide credible evidence to support each answer. This evidence is then verified by the sales leader, and performance is rewarded based on improvement over time.

Even if the Relationship Report Card™ is not used to impact compensation, it is incredibly valuable as a discussion tool for business leaders and sales professionals. A dialogue about each Relationship Report Card™ item, along with actual sales revenue, helps keep the focus on long-term health of a revenue portfolio.

60 Second Actions

- ◆ Put the sales conversation script into practice. Find 3 people this week and use this script to start a conversation with them.
- ◆ Use the Relationship Report Card™ to score yourself.
- ◆ Create a plan for each item on the scorecard and determine what you will do today, this week, and this month to improve your score on each one.
- ◆ Track your self-assessment Relationship Report Card™ score over time and correlate improvement to revenue growth.

Chapter 3

The RaporMax® System

60 Second Summary

In this chapter, you are going to discover the RaporMax® System. This is a tool to help you stay in touch with everyone you've ever met, and it will encourage them to work with you or refer business to you.

This system enables you to use leverage to remind the folks in your natural network how great you are and the value you can provide.

What's in This Chapter for You?

Simply put: Money while you sleep.

The key concept you will discover in this chapter is the leverage your RaporMax® System will create for you to help you automate your communication with everyone you know. Once you set it up, this system will get your prospects ready to work with you and when they reach out to you, you'll be able to complete a sale in 60 seconds.

The system I've created will help people remember you, and it will engage, entertain, and motivate them to reach out to you when they are ready. This chapter is your comprehensive guide to leveraging a lifetime of contacts to have them help you grow your business.

Can Your Grandma Describe What You Do?

If I asked your grandmother what you do, could she tell me? Would she be able to refer me to you? How much detail could she give me about you and what you sell?

You can substitute your best friend, your significant other, one of your kids, or your best client for your grandma. If they can't describe what you do, nobody can.

The case of contractor Don Leonard in Scranton, Pennsylvania, is a great example of this. Don started out as a handyman and apprentice carpenter at age 20. When his grandmother moved into a new home, she had difficulty with some of the standard amenities. Things like steps, bathtub enclosures, and kitchen cabinet height, among other things, became a challenge for her.

In his spare time, Don remodeled his grandmother's home. The work was both functional and aesthetically appealing.

Every time someone visited Don's grandma's house, he received a referral. This gave him the idea to start his own company and focus on remodeling homes based on helping people comply with the building code for people with disabilities.

Don did mailings to people in homes that were over 30 years old and owned by people who were age 60 or older (all of this information was available to him at the local tax assessor's office). In addition, Don developed an email newsletter he sent out each week to local realtors. The newsletter didn't focus as much on what he did, but it kept the real estate professionals up-to-date on the building code, things happening in the community, and how to enhance the value of a home with minor cosmetic modifications.

While Don's grandma was certainly able to describe what he did for a living, most of us do not have as tactile a product or service to distribute to people. Yet it is still incumbent upon us to make sure everyone we know can refer us business.

Your Natural Network

If you were going to host a big birthday party and money was no object, how many people would you invite? Let's say it was a milestone birthday – like your 30th, 40th, or 50th. You can invite your best friends from your childhood, elementary school, high school, college, graduate, and postgraduate school. You can invite your friends from every job you've ever had. You can invite people you interact with socially. You can invite your family and friends. And you can invite everyone with whom you currently do business.

How many people would that be? I'm guessing at least 250 people – most likely more.

Those people I mentioned, everyone with whom you've come into contact, comprise what I call your *natural network*. These are people with whom you've interacted as part of your natural activity.

Imagine the possibilities if you had stayed in touch with those folks over the years. Some of them would be your ideal clients right now. Some of them would have referred you dozens, if not hundreds, of times. Some of them may even have the ability to transform your financial future.

The bad news is, you didn't keep in touch with these folks. As you thumb through your alumni directory, or after attending your high school reunion, or when reconnecting on Facebook with the nerdy guy from science class, you realize that you should have kept in touch with some of them. Although you don't recognize the value most of them could provide, you definitely have missed out on an opportunity because that nerdy guy is now the CEO of a technology company that just went public.

The good news is, it's not too late to rekindle those relationships. As long as they were built on a foundation of trust, you can reconnect with those folks and begin to communicate with them on a regular basis.

There is more good news: You can continue adding people to your natural network. As we go through different stages in life, we continue to make friends and connect with people in meaningful ways. We just need to be certain we value those relationships and never lose touch. Nine times out of ten, these people from your past will be thrilled to hear from you. Once you reconnect, you'll need to stay in touch to rebuild that trust, but, over the long term, these folks will be great referral sources, and some of them will be excellent clients.

In order to reinitiate contact with members of your natural network, you'll need to organize their contact information. This doesn't need to be complicated. You can begin with a simple spreadsheet with the following columns:

◆ Name
◆ Physical address (mailing address)
◆ Email address
◆ Telephone number (I prefer a mobile phone number since people are more likely to answer this number than an office number)
◆ Occupation
◆ Relationship to you (how you know them)
◆ Notes

If you have access to software designed to assist you with the organization of your contacts, that's a plus, but you can easily begin with a simple spreadsheet and import that information into any system you start using in the future.

As your network of contacts grows you will need a client relationship management system to manage this information. Commonly referred to as a CRM system, this software will help keep your list of contacts organized. Eventually, you will begin adding new prospective clients to the list of people in your natural network. This list of contacts is called a "database."

You may be tempted to try to limit the list because you've prejudged the people you know. You've tried to read their minds and assessed their ability to work with you or refer you. Don't do that. Everyone is valuable. Everyone has the ability to refer you.

Here is a guide to help you get your list together. Below is a memory jogger designed to help you compile your list and to keep you honest and make sure you don't forget anyone.

The Natural Network Memory Jogger

GROUP ONE: FRIENDS, NEIGHBORS, AND RELATIVES

These are the people with whom you interact most often. This should be a large list. Start with people you connect with most often and work your way out to friends and relatives you see weekly, monthly, and on holidays.

Relatives

- Parents
- Grandparents
- Siblings
- Cousins
- Aunts and uncles
- In-laws

Neighbors

- People from the street on which you live
- People from around the geographic neighborhood beyond your street
- People whose children go to school with your children
- People from your church or place of worship
- People from the sports teams on which your kids play
- People from the clubs and extracurricular activities to which your kids belong – Boy Scouts, Girl Scouts, 4H, etc.
- Folks from community volunteer groups to which you belong

School Groups – Current and Past

- Classmates and faculty from current educational activities, including trade schools or continuing education courses
- Classmates and faculty from graduate school and postgraduate school
- Classmates and faculty from college
- Classmates and faculty from high school
- Classmates and faculty from elementary school

Note: Use yearbooks, alumni organizations, and social media to connect with them, reconnect with them, and track down their contact information.

GROUP TWO: JOBS, CURRENT AND PAST

- List all bosses, supervisors, anyone with whom you had direct contact over the years.
- Coworkers: Add anyone with whom you worked, shared office space, or anyone within the company with whom you interacted regularly.

- Past clients: Add all past clients and people who worked with your past clients.
- Hot prospects: Add any prospects that you pursued that didn't work out – for whatever reason.

GROUP THREE: RECREATIONAL ACTIVITIES

- People on any team you are a member of: softball, bowling, flag football, volleyball, etc.
- Members of your golf club, tennis club, bridge club, shooting club, etc.
- Social clubs: Any members of specific groups that meet for social activities like the Italian American society (or any society/group that meets regularly)
- Hobby clubs or gatherings: Antique auto clubs, model building, and collectable clubs

GROUP FOUR: PROFESSIONALS

- Doctors
- Dentists
- Pharmacists
- Veterinarians
- Lawyers
- Bankers
- Financial advisors
- CPAs
- Architects
- Teachers
- Clergy
- Therapists
- Consultants
- All office managers and staff from any professional with whom you interact regularly. The staff may be more valuable than the actual principal in many cases.

GROUP FIVE: PEOPLE YOU PAY REGULARLY

- Landscaper
- Swimming pool maintenance company
- Cleaning service – home and office

- Pet groomer
- Barber or hairstylist
- Nail technician
- Massage therapist
- Personal trainer
- Local restaurant owner
- Local shop owner
- Office supply company
- Catering company and food-vending service
- Delivery service
- Copier supplier
- Landlord
- Building maintenance company
- Dry cleaner

GROUP SIX: PEOPLE YOU PAY OCCASIONALLY

- Car dealer
- Jeweler
- Carpenter
- Plumber
- Appliance repair person
- Handyperson or person you call for minor repairs in the home or office
- Painter
- Clothing store owner and custom clothier
- Realtor
- Babysitter and childcare professional
- Rug-cleaning company
- Window-washing company

GROUP SEVEN: OTHER ORGANIZATIONS

- Members of military service organizations
- Members of chamber of commerce
- Members of civic organizations like Rotary, Kiwanis, etc.
- Members of charitable groups or organizations

Note: Be certain to reach out to members in organizations to which you currently belong and people in organizations to which you are a former member.

Reaching Out to Your Network

Once you get your list together, you can begin reaching out to the people on the list. You may not have complete contact information for everyone on the list, but that's fine. Use whatever information you have and begin to reach out to everyone individually.

The initial outreach to everyone in your natural network uses three different forms of contact. We reach out via email, direct mail, and telephone call. Let's face it, some of these folks have not heard from you in a while, so you may need to connect with them a few times before they engage you in conversation.

In addition to three different forms of contact, we also make three attempts with each. Why? Because people typically don't pay attention to anything the first time (or second time) they see it or hear it.

Here are the scripts for each attempt with each form of contact:

EMAIL 1: INITIAL CONTACT
Subject Line: Reconnecting: Remember Me?

Dear <Name>,

It's been a while!

The other day I was thinking back to <when you worked with, went to school with, or last connected with this person> and remembering how much fun we had together. You were always one of the people I respected the most at <name of place you had in common>.

How are you doing?

I'd love to reconnect with you and hear how things are going.

Please reply with a good phone number and time to contact you. I'd really enjoy catching up.

I hope to speak with you soon.

Regards,
Your Name

EMAIL 2: SENT TWO WEEKS AFTER EMAIL ONE
Subject Line: Let's Catch Up: Remember Me?

Dear <Name>,

I've been thinking about you.

The other day I was remembering <when you worked with, went to school with, or last connected with this person> how much fun we had together. You were always one of the people I respected the most at <name of place you had in common>.

I'd love to reconnect and find out how are you doing.

Please reply with a good phone number and time to contact you. I'd really enjoy catching up.

I hope to speak with you soon.

Regards,
Your Name

EMAIL 3: SENT TWO WEEKS AFTER EMAIL TWO
Subject Line: I Miss You. Let's Catch Up

Dear <Name>,

Hope you are well.

I've been thinking about you.

You were always one of the people I respected the most at <name of place you had in common>.

I'd love to reconnect and find out how are you doing.

I'd really enjoy catching up. Reach out to me when you have a chance.

I hope to speak with you soon.

Regards,
Your Name

The sequence for direct mail is similar to the email sequence. The difference is that you include your business card in with the letter.

LETTER 1: INITIAL CONTACT

Put the letter on your letterhead if this is a business letter. If it's a personal letter, a plain white sheet of paper is fine.

Dear <Name>,

It's been a while!

The other day I was thinking back to <when you worked with, went to school with, or last connected with this person> and remembering how much fun we had together. You were always one of the people I respected the most at <name of place you had in common>.

How are you doing?

I'd love to reconnect with you and hear how things are going.

Please call me at your convenience so we can catch up. My phone number is: xxx-xxx-xxxx.

I hope to speak with you soon.

Regards,
Your Name

LETTER 2: SENT TWO WEEKS AFTER LETTER 1

Dear <Name>,

I've been thinking about you.

The other day I was remembering <when you worked with, went to school with, or last connected with this person> how much fun we had together. You were always one of the people I respected the most at <name of place you had in common>.

I'd love to reconnect and find out how are you doing.

Please call me at your convenience so we can catch up. My phone number is: xxx-xxx-xxxx.

I hope to speak with you soon.

Regards,
Your Name

LETTER 3: SENT TWO WEEKS AFTER LETTER 2

Dear <Name>,

Hope you are well.

I've been thinking about you.

You were always one of the people I respected the most at <name of place you had in common>.

I'd love to reconnect and find out how are you doing.

I'd really enjoy catching up. Reach out to me when you have a chance. My telephone number is xxx-xxx-xxxx.

I hope to speak with you soon.

Regards,
Your Name

You should arrange it so the email and direct mail alternate. The full sequence works like this:

Email One – Week one
Direct Mail One – Week two
Email Two – Week three
Direct Mail Two – Week four
Email Three – Week five
Direct Mail Three – Week six

PHONE CALL: WEEK SEVEN

In week seven, you make a telephone call. Here is the script for the call when the person actually answers the phone:

"Hello <name>! It's <your name> from <place where you know them>. It's been a while. How have you been? I'm calling because I've been thinking about you. I was remembering <talk about a time you remember interacting with them>.

Tell me, how have you been? I know we can't catch up on everything that's happened after all this time, but tell me about your family and work."

Then you close the call with:

"It has been great catching up with you. I'd love to stay in touch. Would you mind if I keep you on my VIP contact list? This means you can count on me if you ever need help with anything and you won't feel like a stranger reaching out to me. Is that okay?"

That last part is critical. You are letting them know they can count on you. By implication, you are also asking them if you can count on them. Of course, they will say *yes,* and you'll be able to communicate with them regularly from that point forward.

One thing to remember about this telephone script: You don't only use it in week seven. If at any time the person you are reaching out to calls you, you drop into this script and have this conversation at that time. Of course, you can also suspend the sequence after that, because that was the objective for reaching out in the first place – to renew your relationship and initiate contact.

Voice Mail

If you get voice mail when you make this telephone call, here is a script you can use:

"<Person's name> it's <your name>.

I've been thinking about you a lot lately. Let's catch up. I miss <name something you did together>.

Give me a call: xxx-xxx-xxxx. Looking forward to catching up. It's been too long."

When You Need Money Right Now

Whenever someone comes to me and they are struggling financially, or they are starting a new business, or they've taken on a new sales position, or they just want a boost in their income, I encourage them to call *everyone* in their natural network first.

This means you take the call script and put it both at the beginning and at the end. The phone script and voice mail script are exactly the same. Putting a call in the beginning is a little more aggressive.

During the call, the other person will ask about you and your business. You should highlight the value you provide. Don't be shy. Talk about how you help people. If the other person starts to ask questions, ask if he or she wants help with this aspect of business/life. This could very well turn into a sales opportunity. Remember, the key questions when discussing the value you provide:

"What are your goals?" Or "What are you looking to accomplish in the next year?"

"What does achieving them mean to you personally?" Or "What would accomplishing that mean to you?"

"Would you like some help with that?"

Most often, these calls will serve to help you reconnect with people and begin a process of ongoing communication but, occasionally, direct business or a referral will result.

RaporMax® System for Generating Business While You Sleep

After you reconnect with people in your natural network, you're going to stay in touch with them from now on. The reason: so they will do business with you in the future or refer you to someone who will do business with you.

Think about the most important relationship in your life. It might be the relationship you have with a spouse or significant other. It might be a sibling or a parent. It might be your best friend.

How often do you communicate with that person?

What would happen if you only communicated with that person once a year? Would your relationship get better or worse?

Sometimes when I ask this question while conducting a seminar, someone will say something like:

"I've been with my husband 25 years. The reason we've made it that long is because we haven't spoken to each other in the past 19..."

While that's funny, we all know frequency of communication builds trust.

That's why I created the RaporMax® System (Figure 3.1). This is your sales operating system. It helps you continuously follow up with everyone you know, until they die (or opt out).

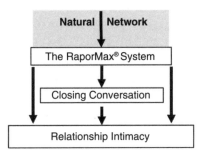

FIGURE 3.1 The RaporMax® System

The list of contacts you've organized is technically called a database. Even if it's a simple spreadsheet, it is now a tool for you to use to help sell yourself, your products, and the experience you provide.

Everyone on your list is now in your database, even the people who didn't respond to your email, letters, or telephone calls. I'm going to repeat that because it's an important point. Everyone goes into your database – even if you didn't connect with them – unless they specifically asked you to never contact them again.

People get busy. Many of them wanted to reach out to you but their day-to-day activities got the better of them and they didn't make time for the conversation they knew they would have with you.

Your goal with the RaporMax® System is to educate, entertain, and remind people of the value you provide. When we do this, we also want to motivate them to call you when they have a problem you can solve or when they want help from you in achieving a goal.

This system will help you take advantage of some of the most effective levers of communication. They are:

♦ Primacy
♦ Recency
♦ Frequency
♦ Emotional resonance

People are influenced by the first thing they hear on any given subject. If I told you Dr. Smith was the best cosmetic surgeon in your local area and that was the first thing you heard about Dr. Smith, anyone saying anything to the contrary would have to overcome the hurdle of your perception of this doctor as "the best."

The same holds true for any idea you introduce to your natural network.

This is the effect of primacy.

People are often influenced by the last thing they hear before they make a decision. If you are in the market for a new car and immediately before visiting the dealership, you ask your next-door neighbors how they like the vehicle they have, you'll be predisposed to select that vehicle – as long as the review was positive.

Being influenced by the last thing you experience is called the recency effect.

One of the most powerful influences in communication is frequency. The more a message is repeated, the more you see it and hear it, the greater the influence it has on you. That's the main reason advertisers play the same commercials over and over again. The message penetrates your conscious mind and becomes embedded into your subconscious.

Frequency of communication builds trust.

The final element of persuasive communication you leverage in the RaporMax® System is emotional resonance. This is the connection you make with your audience through stories that evoke emotion. Anytime you move an audience member to have an emotional reaction – laugh, cry, hope, fear, even smile – you have connected with them. When they feel the same emotion you (or the lead character of your story) felt, you have bonded.

All four of these elements are present in every message you send through the RaporMax® System.

Here's how the system works:

Each week you are going to send an article to everyone in your database via email. The email will leverage the four elements of persuasive communication we discussed and it will educate, entertain, and continue to deepen your relationship with them.

Once each month you're going to send a printed newsletter to everyone in your audience. The print newsletter can be a compilation of the four articles you've sent out from the previous weeks or it can be completely original content.

Twice each year, you're going to reach out and call everyone on your list. You can rotate these folks throughout the course of the year but you need to try to make voice contact with them at least two times each 12-month period.

The system is elegant in its simplicity, and it is stunningly effective.

Keep the simplicity of the idea in mind, because there are dozens of ways to make it more complicated. The key is to stick to the schedule. The frequency of the interaction with your audience is the most important element. The variety of contact will also increase the likelihood of engagement.

Weekly Email Newsletter

Select a dedicated system to send your weekly email. There are a number of email marketing systems that exist solely to send out mass email communication. Select the one you find easiest to use and load your contacts into it.

Each week, create a unique article that educates, entertains, and connects with your audience. Send the email on the same day and time each week. The consistency is important because it demonstrates your reliability.

The topics you select will be based on a content calendar you create. Set up the topics in a five-week rotation to keep your audience interested.

Here is a sample topic rotation:

Week 1: Personal story or life lesson

Week 2: Share your opinion of a topic that is in the news

Week 3: Educate your audience on an industry topic

Week 4: Book review, movie review, or restaurant review

Week 5: A promotional email for your services

Each five weeks, these topics repeat.

When I teach this process to professionals in a business-to-business sales role, they always ask about the topic rotation. One of the biggest questions is: "Why would my audience want to hear about a movie review from me? Can't I just talk about my business and what I do each week?"

Your audience is made up of people. While your business is interesting to you, people will not want to hear about it every week, and eventually, the bulk of them will tune you out. You vary the topics so there is always something new and interesting for them to discover.

The number-one selling magazine in the world is a supermarket checkout counter gossip magazine. Television shows that offer a glimpse of how people live and the drama associated with their lives are always highly rated.

People like to live vicariously through others. They like the voyeuristic element of going behind the scenes into the lives of someone else – yes, even business people enjoy this.

Let's break down each of these types of articles so you have a better idea of what the content should be and how it connects to your audience.

WEEK ONE: THE PERSONAL STORY OR LIFE LESSON

This is an article that demonstrates some vulnerability on your part. You discuss how you made a mistake or did something foolish and what you learned from it. This may seem counterintuitive because you want to build up your credibility with your audience. But you don't demonstrate vulnerability in your work. You demonstrate vulnerability as a human being.

Examples of Successful Topics

Title/Subject line: How I Got So Fat – In this article I discuss how I gained weight because my focus wasn't on my health. I was working so much I took shortcuts on the thing that was most important. The lesson was to not take shortcuts on things that are most important to your success.

Title/Subject line: My Most Embarrassing Moment and What You Can Learn from It – This was an article about how I accidentally went into a women's studies class in college and made a fool of myself because I wouldn't ask for directions. The lesson was to ask for help when you need it.

Title/Subject line: What I Learned about Success from My Two-Year-Old – In this article, I talked about how life was so simple for my son when he was age 2. We only make life complicated later on. The lesson was that business can be the same way.

Each time I share a little bit of personal vulnerability with the audience, they can relate to me more and more. The idea is that this is a conversation we're having across the kitchen table.

WEEK TWO: SHARE YOUR OPINION ON SOMETHING THAT IS IN THE NEWS

People don't have to agree with your opinion; in fact, it's better if they don't, but they'll respect you for sharing your thoughts.

The subjects and topics for this type of email article should be "ripped from the headlines." Focus on things in the news that your ideal clients are angry about or frustrated with.

Share your opinion on these things and watch the feedback come rolling in.

WEEK THREE: EDUCATE YOUR AUDIENCE ON AN INDUSTRY TOPIC

This is your opportunity to demonstrate your expertise in your industry. Help your readers discover something new and interesting about what you do. Here are some ideas based on industry:

- ◆ Car Mechanic: Five Ways to Extend the Life of Your Tires
- ◆ Dentist: How to Whiten Your Teeth at Home in Fifteen Minutes
- ◆ Real Estate Agent: Five Reasons to Have a Home Inspection before You Make an Offer
- ◆ Pharmaceutical Sales Representative: Time Saving Tips from the Best Medical Office Managers
- ◆ Private Jet Company Sales Executive: Seven Things Aircraft Fleet Managers Do to Keep Maintenance Budgets in Line
- ◆ Copier Sales Manager: Three Ways to Keep Your Office Supply Budget in Line in an Economic Downturn

Those ideas are some of the most successful emails (as determined by number of leads generated) that my clients have used over the years.

WEEK FOUR: BOOK REVIEW, MOVIE REVIEW, OR RESTAURANT REVIEW

This topic week you are going to share some thoughts on a leisure activity. Again, you are connecting on a human level with people. You want to showcase the commonality you all share. One five-week cycle you can review a book. Five weeks later, you can share a family recipe. Five weeks after that, you can review a restaurant.

One of the most successful emails a real estate attorney client of mine ever sent was titled: "My Secret System for How to Keep Pancakes Warm." The calls flooded into his office asking about this system and how it worked. While people were on the telephone, the lawyer was able to remind the callers (many of whom were real estate brokers and agents) of the quality of his work. He wound up having a record month.

Week Five: A Promotional Email for Your Services

Every five weeks you are going to make a direct offer to your audience. This could be an offer to help them solve a problem or to help them achieve a goal. It could be an offer of a special service based upon the time of the year.

The main goal of this particular email is to keep people focused on the value you provide.

Every five weeks, you are going to repeat this sequence with new articles but similar themes. Over and over again.

About 20% to 30% of the people in your database will read these emails. Those are the folks we care about. They are open to a relationship with you. You might communicate with them for years before they reach out and call you.

Each week, some people will unsubscribe from your email list. This will bother you at first, but you must realize that people who unsubscribe are people who would, most likely, never be good clients for you. This is because the weekly email is like an ongoing conversation, and if these folks have decided they don't want to be a part of that conversation, you definitely don't want them around.

At some point, you will think your business is different. You'll think this content calendar is not sophisticated enough for your audience. Or you might think that emailing them weekly will be too bothersome. Or you might be persuaded by some company to have a "professional" write your email.

Don't give in to any of those temptations.

The way you write is the way you think. If someone else writes these newsletters, you will have outsourced your thinking to someone else. You might be an entrepreneur and the proprietor of a $20 million business or you may work for a large company, or even a small company, representing products and services with a fantastic reputation that people buy from you. These newsletters need to be your words and your thinking.

In addition, this content mix, delivered with this frequency, written by you, is the recipe for maximum success. I've seen it work in the most sophisticated professional settings (engineers, attorneys, cosmetic surgeons, etc.).

The minute you deviate from the success formula as it is outlined, you decrease the effectiveness of the solution. It's like adding water to an alcoholic beverage. You may get the desired result eventually but it won't work as quickly or with as much potency.

Your monthly print newsletter can be one of the weekly email articles you are particularly proud of or it can be all four of those articles put together into a traditional newsletter format. You can write the newsletter in the format of a regular letter if you'd like. The idea is to get information in the mail and into the hands of the members of your audience once each month.

The reason a print newsletter is effective is because it connects with people who do not read email. You'll find a certain segment of your audience will only respond to the physical letters you send.

The United States Postal Service is not as overwhelmed these days compared to a couple of decades ago. It is effective at delivering your newsletters, and people will notice them and read them. Do not skip this step, even if you only select a small segment of your audience due to the expense of printing and postage.

The final element is the biannual call to everyone on your list. If you have a large list, break it down to 10 to 20 calls per day. You'll only reach about 5% to 10% of the people you call, but you'll leave voicemail messages for the rest of them.

Use the same script we described earlier. This script for both the call and the voicemail works because it is focused on the person on the other end of the phone. You are demonstrating your external orientation and showing people how much you care.

Once you begin communicating with everyone in your natural network on a regular basis, you'll be amazed at the referrals and new business opportunities that surface. If you have a large natural network, you may be able to achieve your growth goals for the year just from implementing this system.

In our next chapter, we are going to focus on adding more people to your natural network. That is the key to sustainable long-term growth. As new people come into your business and your life, you immediately add them to the RaporMax® System and let it work its magic. You utilize leverage to connect with your audience over and over until one day someone calls you and asks for help.

60 Second Actions

- ◆ Organize your natural network into a spreadsheet with all contact information.
- ◆ Reach out to everyone and make the initial contact.
- ◆ Set up your RaporMax® System with weekly email, monthly newsletters, and biannual phone calls.
- ◆ Create your first five weeks of content in your content calendar.
- ◆ Set the system in motion.

Chapter 4

Get MAD, Get Clients, Get Money

60 Second Summary

This chapter will help you look at your ideal client in a way you never imagined. You will discover a method for fine-tuning a message that will resonate with them and motivate them to act – meaning reach out to you for help. You'll also get a jump start on discovering how you can put this message in front of your ideal client over and over again, in a systematic way.

If you've ever had a bad sales meeting when you thought you and your prospective client were speaking a different language, this chapter will be of great value.

If you've ever left a client meeting and thought to yourself: "I wish I had 20 clients like that person," this chapter will make your day.

If you value opportunities to connect with multiple prospects at one time, this chapter will change your business forever.

What's in This Chapter for You?

More clients just like your best client.

The key concept you will discover in this chapter is an interview called the Ideal Relationship Targeting 21 or IRT 21. This 21 question interview is to be conducted with your best clients and it will help you create a message that will resonate with them and target other prospective clients just like them, in large numbers.

When you know how to target prospective clients who are identical to your best client, you have leverage. This means your life as a business leader and sales professional is about to get much, much easier.

Match the Message to the Audience

In some of the most economically challenged neighborhoods in the United States, people are running to file their taxes.

In January 2010 I met a CPA entrepreneur named Noreen. She had just leased office space, set up her desk, and hung her shingle. She accepted a severance package from a large firm in December and was eager to make her mark on the world.

Noreen's goal was to become the CPA business owners would love. She believed most CPAs were not providing enough guidance and support to their clients. Noreen thought CPAs should be helping small business clients with everything from evaluating equipment financing options to structuring compensation agreements for minimizing tax exposure.

The problem: She had no clients.

Noreen grew up in Miami and speaks English, Spanish, and Creole fluently. This positioned her perfectly to serve the diverse community.

At our first meeting, Noreen clarified the goal for our work together: Get enough clients in the door to have positive cash flow by the summer. I was skeptical until Noreen shared a story with me.

"My parents owned a business and they loved paying their taxes. I know that sounds strange, but when every penny you bring in goes toward paying bills, your tax refund is a welcome windfall. Each January, when the W-2 forms (wage statements detailing how much an employee was paid) would show up in our mailbox, my parents would rush down to the local franchise tax prep company and get our taxes done – so we could get the refund. These places offered an advance on your tax return and you could walk in with forms and walk out with money."

Immediately, Noreen and I reached out to community leaders in middle class and economically challenged neighborhoods. Our message: "Come in and get the cash the government owes you. Bring your W-2 form from your employer, we will do your taxes, and give you the refund you're owed – on the spot."

As people came into the office, Noreen made note of the local employers and sent letters to each one. These letters had a different message. This message was:

"We are the entrepreneur's CPA. Having grown up as the daughter of two business owners, I know the challenges of doing payroll, evaluating equipment purchases, and securing financing for growth. I want to help you use financial information to make better decisions. The next time your CPA says you can't do something, call me and together we will figure out how you can!"

Just three short years later, Noreen was doing taxes for over 2,500 families, but she was also known as "the entrepreneur's CPA," with over 400 business clients.

How did Noreen make that happen?

She focused on matching her message to the different audience groups. Her tax return message resonated with consumers and her business friendly message connected with small business owners.

Matching your message to your audience is the first part of a three-letter acronym that will make all the difference in developing relationships. That acronym: MAD.

It stands for:

Message

Audience

Delivery system

I love helping people get MAD. It is the one thing that most people don't understand when they attempt to start and deepen relationships with prospective clients.

Getting MAD, and even obsessing over it, is helpful for relationships.

Now, if you thought I was advocating screaming and yelling as a strategy, well, that may have some applicability as a delivery method for certain audiences, but the acronym makes it easy to remember how everything works in alignment.

This concept is critical because different groups of people respond to different messages. The response of the message recipient depends on several factors:

◆ Who they are
◆ Their background

- Their role in the organization or in the group making the purchase
- How they feel about life, business, and the sales process
- The people around them who have influence over their decisions
- Any training they have had in your area of expertise
- Their level of sophistication as a buyer

There is an expression people often use to describe great sales professionals: "That person could sell ice to an Eskimo."

While this is descriptive, it highlights everything that's wrong with old-school sales.

The message doesn't match the audience. The sales pro mentioned in the quote might be good enough to sell one block of ice after approaching 10 Eskimos, but if they approached 10 Hawaiians with the ice, they'd probably go 8 for 10.

It's easier to sell ice to people who are hot. It's even easier to sell ice to people who are hot and have purchased ice before. It is easier still to sell ice to people who are hot, have purchased ice before, and are looking for a new person to supply them with ice.

The powerful idea behind the 60 Second Sale is: if someone is ready, willing, and able to buy from you, and they know you, like you, and trust you, it should only take 60 seconds to close the deal.

That's why we are going to invest time finding people who fit those criteria.

How to Find People Who Will Say YES to a Deal

Take a few minutes and think about all the clients you've worked with during your career. Think about everyone who has purchased from you. Now, mentally separate the clients who were the absolute best. What do they all have in common?

They all:

- Treat you as a peer
- Value your opinion
- Trust that you are always focused on their best interest (have an external orientation)

- ◆ Remain loyal to you and your business
- ◆ Have a high lifetime value

When you are developing a sales message, you develop it for these people – your ideal clients. When I present this concept to an audience, someone always raises a hand and says, "Well, sure Dave, but those people are one in a million."

The reason you feel these people are so rare is because you have not focused on them. You've spent your entire career focused on attracting "ANY" client and not your "IDEAL" client.

Think about it this way: It is rare to see a blue car on the road. According to the two companies that manufacture auto paint for vehicles produced in the United States, blue cars make up only 7% of the total produced each year. Yet, now that I've shared that statistic with you, you'll see several blue cars today.

Why?

Because you are focused on finding blue cars.

The same thing is true for clients. If you focus on finding ideal clients, you'll be absolutely amazed when they begin dropping out of the sky and landing on your desk.

If you want to start relationships with people who are identical to your best clients, you need to have a message that resonates with them. This means you must find out what motivates them emotionally.

What would make them get up off the couch and run outside in a snowstorm just for a chance to do business with you?

To motivate someone in that way you have to:

- ◆ Have as targeted and focused a message as possible
- ◆ Solve a problem or help achieve a goal
- ◆ Enter the conversation they are having around their kitchen table

Once you have a profile of your ideal client, you need to find more people just like them and begin the process of demonstrating your value. This requires an in-depth look at each of these folks. The starting point for this analysis is to understand the way your ideal client thinks and what that client feels.

Reach out to a handful of your ideal clients and ask if you can interview them. Your focus is to understand them so you can enter the conversations taking place around their kitchen tables.

In order to identify the ideal audience of clients, we need to find points of commonality among them.

For this purpose, I've developed a list of questions I call the *IRT 21*. That is an acronym for "Ideal Relationship Targeting 21."

These 21 questions will help you do a number of things:

◆ Identify points of commonality among your best clients.
◆ Create messaging to resonate with them.
◆ Target locations, events, and groups where they congregate.
◆ Find media that will allow you to deliver your message to the target audience in an effective way.

We start with a broad focus and narrow our questions down so we can be as specific as possible. This allows us to really get MAD. This means we:

◆ Craft a **m**essage that will resonate
◆ Identify the ideal client – our **a**udience.
◆ Identify the appropriate **d**elivery system to get the message to the audience.

IRT 21

1. Do most of your ideal clients belong to one industry/tribe?
2. Who is the most recognizable ambassador for this group?
3. Who are the emerging leaders of the group?
4. What is their average transaction size (when they sell their products/services)?
5. What is their average investment with you (or a business in your industry)?
6. What do they worry about most?
7. What are they angry about?
8. What are their major frustrations?
9. What do they secretly desire?
10. Is there a preference to the way they make decisions?

11. Do they have their own language?
12. Who has tried to sell to them and failed?
13. Who is working with them successfully?
14. What in the economy has an impact on them?
15. What industry trends are currently impacting them?
16. What do they read?
17. What organizations do they belong to? Where do they gather?
18. What lists might they be on?
19. Who do they trust?
20. Is there a media outlet they prefer?
21. Is there seasonality to their behavior?

Let's break down each of these questions and determine why they are so effective:

Question 1: Do most of your ideal clients belong to one industry/tribe?

If you were to start your business from scratch, today, your first client would be your most important client. You'd want to know everything about them. Arguably the most important thing to discover is: What groups do they belong to?

The reason this is so important: If you solve a problem for one person, you can solve it for many people. Your clients want to work with people who have experience in the same industry or tribe. (I use this word to identify groups of people gathered for a common purpose. For example, stamp collectors, parents of children who take ballet lessons, golf enthusiasts, and folks who raise chinchillas are all members of a tribe.)

Question 2: Who is the most recognizable ambassador for this group?

Every group has someone taking a high profile to champion the causes it holds dear. Some groups have many people in this role.

Sometimes this will be a media personality and other times it will be a celebrity only in the circles of the group members – like the president of a trade association or industry education group. Your goal is to find out who this "ambassador" is and research everything about them.

Question 3: Who are the emerging leaders of the group?

Most groups have awards or ways of recognizing people who are rising stars. Just like with the ambassadors, you need to know who these people are and find out everything there is to know about them.

If your best clients are trying to emulate the business and lifestyle practices of these people, you need to make sure you are familiar with those practices.

Question 4: What is their average transaction size (when they sell their products/services)?

How much revenue do they bring in per transaction? People who sell country club memberships, jewelry, and private jets have a different average transaction size when compared with people who sell shoes, retail cleaning supplies, and sandwiches. This fact dictates an approach to market that is dramatically different.

Question 5: What is their average investment with you (or a business in your industry)?

Some prospective clients have better access to financial resources and have specific needs for large quantities of your product or service.

Question 6: What do they worry about most?

Is something keeping them awake at night? If they could change one thing about their business or their life, what would it be?

Question 7: What are they angry about?

An easy answer for business-to-business clients is regulation. Every business owner thinks there is too much of it, and that it is stifling growth.

Think beyond the obvious. What else might they be angry about? Dig deep into this, because it is helpful in crafting a message.

Question 8: What are their major frustrations?

Again, here you'll see commonality across all industries for certain things – like paperwork, rising energy costs, etc. Dig deep and uncover some specific things your best clients have in common.

Question 9: What do they secretly desire?

This is a difficult answer to pin down. The best way for me to help you understand the value of this question is to give you an example from the world of professional speaking.

These days, anyone can become a professional speaker. You simply have to have the guts to get up in front of a group of people and talk. That's it.

When you ask anyone just starting out in this profession, "What do you secretly desire?" they will say they want to be the next Anthony Robbins or John Maxwell or Zig Ziglar.

Understanding this desire is helpful because people will emulate their heroes and you can develop a message accordingly.

Question 10: Is there a preference to the way they make decisions?

If you have ever pitched to an executive who was a McKinsey alumnus (a former consultant with McKinsey & Company) you know they make decisions through a process called MECE – seeking mutually exclusive and collectively exhaustive options. This process attempts to remove emotion and make decisions based on cold hard facts.

Certain industries have generally accepted principles they follow. You need to uncover these and leverage them in your messaging.

Question 11: Do they have their own language?

Have you ever eavesdropped on a conversation between police officers? They have a way of speaking that is unique to their profession.

Wall Street traders also have a language of their own, as do car salespeople and diamond dealers and just about any other industry and tribe. Learn the language, but be careful using it. You can drop an occasional word and look like you're making an effort, but overuse of specific terms will make you seem like a fraud.

Question 12: Who has tried to sell to them and failed?

Who didn't earn their trust? Who has given up on them? Why?

Question 13: Who is working with them successfully?
Who is successfully providing value to them? What is so valuable about this solution? Why do they like it so much?

Question 14: What in the economy has an impact on them?
Are there some economic forces applying pressure to them or their business? For example: Interest rates have a huge impact on real estate sales.

Question 15: What industry trends are currently impacting them?
What is going on within their industry? How is it affecting them? What will happen if this factor changes?

Question 16: What do they read?
Do they read a specific news publication? Do they subscribe to a trade magazine? Is there an informational website they visit regularly? Do they all use a specific app on their phones?

You want to know this: (1) so you can read it too, and (2) so you can submit articles for publication.

Question 17: What organizations do they belong to? Where do they gather?
Similar to question 16, you want to go to the conventions they attend and eventually become a speaker at these gatherings.

Question 18: What lists might they be on?
You want to find a way to target them with your message. If they are all on a specific list, it makes it easier to reach out en masse.

Question 19: Who do they trust?
There is always one person (and sometimes more than one) every group relates to and invests their trust in. You need to find out who that person is for your group of ideal clients.

For example:

People who are politically conservative in the United States trust radio talk show host Rush Limbaugh.

In the 1960s and 1970s Walter Cronkite, the anchor of *CBS Evening News,* was regarded as the most trusted man in America.

Question 20: Is there a media outlet they prefer?
Each of us has the option to now choose our flavor of cable news. In addition, there are subcategories of channels appearing

on satellite television and radio all the time. Your ideal clients have a preference. Find out what it is.

Question 21: Is there a seasonality to their behavior?

Some businesses only set their budgets in October for a fiscal year beginning on January 1. If you don't have a place in the budget, you cannot get hired. You better target these businesses in the summer and early fall.

Identifying seasonality will help you marshal your resources appropriately when you need to influence a decision.

Adjust the wording of the questions so they apply to an individual business and initiate a conversation with an ideal client. You may not be able to get through all of these questions in one telephone call, but developing a profile over time for each of your best clients and then comparing them to each other will help identify commonality and that will help with your message targeting.

Delivery System

The final element in the MAD formula is the delivery system.

A delivery system is the way the message reaches the target audience. If you are selling something to another person – belly-to-belly – you are the delivery system since they get the message directly from you.

The challenge with belly-to-belly selling is the lack of leverage. You can only personally meet with a finite number of people in any given day. This stacks the odds against you. Even if your message is perfect and you've selected the ideal audience, your timing might not be right and the time you invest with that individual may not result in a sale.

That's why I recommend using high-leverage delivery systems to get your message in front of people and help them recognize your value.

That's the focus of our next chapter.

60 Second Actions

◆ Immediately make a list of your best clients. Pick one from each group and interview them using the IRT 21. Repeat this process until you find the commonality among your best clients.

◆ Use the interview information to develop messages that resonate with each of those groups. Test the messaging by going back to the clients with the messages you uncovered in your client interviews. When you look at the data you've compiled, you'll find that you have a few great messages, a profile of your ideal client, and two or three delivery systems that will get your message in front of the ideal client over and over again.

◆ Examine how each of your ideal clients found you. What delivery system connected them to you? Look for other message delivery systems they may have in common. Do they all read a particular publication? Do they all attend a specific convention each year?

◆ Commonality among clients is the key to identifying great delivery systems. Make lists of all the points of commonality.

Chapter 5

Forget the Frat Boy Approach – Convert with a Honeypot

60 Second Summary

In this chapter, we discuss how you take people who look and act like your best clients, introduce yourself to them, and get them to show an interest in the value you provide.

You uncover the four groups of people who have an impact on every decision you make in your business.

I introduce the six client attraction systems designed to help you leverage your time and the investment of your financial resources as you grow your revenue.

You are introduced to the conversion process and given a step-by-step guide to move people through the client life cycle and into a relationship with you.

You discover my proprietary tool for converting strangers into prospective clients. This is called a *honeypot,* and it will change the way you view selling.

What's in This Chapter for You?

This is the chapter that ends cold calling for you forever. After reading this portion of the 60 Second Sale, you will be able to present yourself as an expert providing priceless guidance.

The key concept you will discover in this chapter is called a honeypot. This is something you offer to a group of suspects to pique their interest in beginning a relationship with you (see Figure 5.2).

This concept will help differentiate you from your competitors and allow you to command a fee premium.

Know the People in Your Database

In late June 2009, I came to an important realization. My business was eight months old and I had finished calling everyone in my natural network. I added everyone from my natural network into my RaporMax® System. The system was working. I received an occasional referral, but the revenue was inconsistent. I needed to increase the number of people in my database. Don't get me wrong, I was grateful for the referrals my family, friends, and acquaintances sent me, but since most of them weren't my ideal clients, the business generated from this group alone was not sufficient.

It was time for me to examine my natural network, figure out which relationships were most valuable, and create a plan for replicating them. There were about 500 people in my database, and each of them was receiving my weekly email and monthly direct mail newsletters.

Since most of these people were relationships I had developed through my daily life activities, they were not organized in any particular way. The only thing they had in common was a relationship with me. I began to examine each relationship, one by one, and what I found changed my approach forever.

After completing my relationship review, I realized there were four groups of people I needed to focus on to grow my business.

The first group contained the most valuable people on my list. They were people who paid me for the value I provided. Some of them paid me significant fees for consulting services and others paid to attend a seminar or educational event I hosted. Some of these people were so happy with the results they received that they referred me to other people. I labeled this group CLIENTS.

This next category of people were folks who had never paid me for my services but referred business to me. They trusted me enough to recommend me to others. They were out in the world introducing me to people and bringing them into my office to do business with me. I called these people EVANGELISTS.

The third group of people on my list were people who expressed interest in the work I did and the value I provided, but they had not yet invested in my services. These folks had the potential to become clients. They were prospective clients. I labeled them PROSPECTS.

These three groups of people all knew me and had expressed some level of interest in me and the value I provided. The first two groups – clients and evangelists – trusted me enough to invest money in me or recommend me to others.

After conducting this review, I realized I needed to grow the number of people in my network – not with just anyone, but with people who had the same qualities as my ideal clients. I reached out to my clients and conducted an IRT 21 interview with each of them. This helped me develop a profile of my ideal clients, create solid messages that resonated with them, and discover some clues about where they could be found. I named the people in this target group SUSPECTS because I suspected they could be good clients because they possessed the same characteristics as many of my ideal clients.

My mission became getting my message in front of as many of these suspects as possible. Over the course of the next five years, through trial and error, I discovered six ways to attract people I suspected would be good clients. These six activities, when combined with my RaporMax® system, make up the seven message delivery systems that start and build lifelong, high-value client relationships.

These message delivery systems will fuel your growth, drive qualified prospects directly to your door, and make you lots of money.

The seven systems are:

Sales Operating System: The RaporMax® System. Everyone you've ever met and everyone you will meet is immediately entered into it. You start it up with people in your natural network and it grows over time with folks you suspect will someday become ideal clients. This system is the key to closing deals, deepening relationships, and skyrocketing lifetime value.

Client Attraction System One: Speaking. This is a system for developing new relationships when you give a presentation to a group of people.

Client Attraction System Two: Publishing. This is a system for when you publish an article.

Client Attraction System Three: Networking. This is a system for when you meet with new people either one-on-one or at an event.

Client Attraction System Four: Primary Internet Presence. This is a system for leveraging your website.

Client Attraction System Five: Social Media. This is a system to take advantage of the modern town square.

Client Attraction System Six: ACTION^{TM} Advertising. This is a system to make every ad provide a return on investment with or without a huge budget.

The RaporMax® System is our sales operating system. Everyone we meet goes into this system and receives a weekly email and a monthly print newsletter. We communicate with them often. The reason we do this is to get them to take action. We want prospects to take action and become clients. We want clients to deepen their relationships with us, and we want evangelists to refer us more frequently.

A client can deepen his/her relationship with us in three ways:

1. Invest in a higher value product or service.
2. Invest in our product or service more frequently.
3. Introduce us to someone else who will invest in our product or service (see Figure 5.1).

The six other systems serve as an introduction to us and a gateway to a relationship. We use those six systems – speaking, publishing, networking, primary internet presence, social media, and ACTION™ advertising – to target suspects, convert them into prospects, and then enter them into our RaporMax® System.

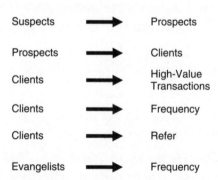

Suspects	→	Prospects
Prospects	→	Clients
Clients	→	High-Value Transactions
Clients	→	Frequency
Clients	→	Refer
Evangelists	→	Frequency

Figure 5.1   Conversion Actions

Round Up the Suspects and Convert Them

Once you've identified a group of suspects, you cannot simply run up to each of them and say, "Hey, let's work together!" Actually, you can, but that would take a massive amount of time and you'd receive lots of rejection.

People move out of the category of suspect when they take action.

The relationship between you and a suspect is almost nonexistent. You believe, based on your targeting, this person will have a problem you can solve or a goal you can help achieve. Currently, the suspect doesn't know you, like you, or trust you. The suspect might not even know you exist. You have selected that person but he or she has not made any effort to develop a relationship with you.

You have to change that.

So you reach out to these suspects and begin to communicate with them. If they are receptive to your communication, they move from being a suspect to becoming a prospect. That conversion from suspect to prospect is based on active interest on the part of the individual with whom you are communicating.

It is analogous to dating. Imagine that there is a "special someone" you are romantically interested in. That person is perfect in every way, with the physical qualities you find appealing. This person is your intellectual equal and you cross paths frequently. At that point, that person is a dating suspect.

One day you walk up to this amazing individual and say, "Would you like to get a cup of coffee with me?"

If the answer is yes, the person has become a dating prospect. You have the cup of coffee to determine if you'd like to spend more time together developing a relationship.

Think about a different scenario. Imagine you saw that person as an ideal dating suspect. What would happen if you asked the person to go directly to bed with you? Well, 99 times out of 100, you'd get slapped in the face, but maybe just once, someone would take you up on this offer. That is a horrible success rate because your approach is horrible.

In the process, you'd irreparably damage 99 relationships and never be permitted to communicate with those people again.

You were forcing a level of intimacy upon them that made them uncomfortable.

I call this the frat boy approach because when I was in college, a particular fraternity would require its members to perform this crude ritual – approach 100 women and ask them to go directly to bed. This resulted in a horrible reputation on campus for its members.

About half of those women would have responded favorably to the invitation for coffee. The relationships that didn't progress beyond coffee would remain in good standing in the event the circumstances changed, or the women would at least be open to additional communication in the future.

The frat boy approach is the one chosen by most sales professionals today. They have no relationship with the people they suspect will be good clients, yet they come on fast and strong and ask for a significant commitment before getting to know the prospective client and his/her goals.

Our approach is better. Once we've identified the audience of people who are like our ideal clients, we label them suspects.

Then we make them an appropriate offer to develop a relationship. We do this via our six client attraction systems: speaking, publishing, networking, our primary internet presence, social media, or ACTION™ advertising. The people who accept our offer have converted from suspects into prospects.

We then communicate with prospects through the RaporMax® System in order to convert them into clients.

The six client attraction systems are like our cup of coffee and the RaporMax® System is dating.

Once they become clients, we continue that communication through the RaporMax® System in order to get them to:

- ◆ Buy from us more frequently.
- ◆ Invest more money per transaction.
- ◆ Refer other people to us.

Let's review each of these audience groups and our goals during our communication with them.

SUSPECTS

These are people we believe have the qualities of our best clients. We have one goal in communicating with them. That goal is to convert them into prospects.

We identify suspects by building a profile through the Ideal Relationship Targeting 21 process and then looking for groups of people who fit that profile. Once we've identified those groups, we try to deliver presentations to them via speaking engagements, write articles for them via publications, network with them, advertise to them, and connect with them via referrals and social media.

We use the six client attraction systems to convert suspects into prospects.

PROSPECTS

The term *prospect* is short for "prospective client." Prospects are people who have demonstrated some interest in working with us. Most often, this interest is when they request information we have on a specific subject.

Our goal with prospects is to continue to communicate with them through the RaporMax® System and convert them into clients.

CLIENTS

Clients are people who have invested money in us or in our products and services. People convert from prospects into clients when they pay us.

I'm often asked why I use the word *client* and not the word *customer*. A client is someone who buys from an individual based upon a relationship. A customer is someone who buys from a business or a vending machine – the focus is on transactions. We focus on relationships, and that's why we have clients.

We have three goals in continuing to communicate with clients:

1. Invest in us more frequently.
2. Invest in us at a higher value for each transaction.
3. Refer us to other people with whom we can do business.

EVANGELISTS

Evangelists are people who have never used our products or services but continue to refer us.

Evangelists are highly valuable for the following reasons:

◆ *They drive business directly to your doorstep.* Most evangelists will connect you with people who are ready, willing, and able to do business with you. This happens because the trust the new client places in the evangelist is transferred to you. That trust is like gold. It would take an enormous amount of time to develop if you were even able to do it on your own.

◆ *Referrals from evangelists are a low-cost way to attract clients.* When you compare the expense of a referral from an evangelist to the cost of a client sourced from advertising, the difference is amazing. Your investment in your evangelist relationships comes in the form of ongoing communication and in referring business to them.

◆ *Evangelists enhance your leverage.* You can have dozens or even hundreds of evangelists working to refer you clients. These people are like an army of sales professionals out on the street looking to send new clients your way. Your investment of time and attention in them is repaid by this dedication.

◆ *Evangelists help build your credibility with groups of suspects.* If you are looking to write articles or speak to groups of suspects, your community of evangelists can help you attract those opportunities. As with direct referrals, these strategic opportunities develop from the evangelist relationship because the trust people have in the evangelist is transferred to you through their referral.

How to Identify Evangelists Evangelists cannot be targeted directly. You'll find that people often become evangelists as a way of "giving back" to you for something you've done for them. For example: Many people who read my books or attend my speaking engagements refer others to me over and over without ever doing business directly with me.

They are evangelists for me because they derive so much value from my books and speeches that they wholeheartedly believe in what I am doing. Yet for whatever reason, the timing is not right for them to invest in a relationship with me.

The way to identify evangelists is to continue to communicate with them as if they are prospects and continue to deliver valuable information to them through your RaporMax® System.

Here's an example of an evangelist relationship: Steve Klitzner is a friend of mine. He has a unique law firm. Steve's exclusive focus is on solving problems that people have with the Internal Revenue Service. That's all he does. That is the expertise he and his team possess.

Fortunately for me, I've never had a problem with the IRS. But I've referred dozens of people to Steve over the years. Is it because he is great at what he does? Yes. Is it because I like him? Absolutely. Is it because I know he will treat everyone I send over to him with the care and concern he would use if he were working with me? Definitely.

My relationship with Steve is so valuable to me that I have gone to speaking engagements and delivered presentations on his behalf. It is so valuable to me that I'm mentioning him in this book.

But I've never used his services because I haven't had the need.

That makes me an evangelist for Steve.

There are people who are evangelists for you. Think about them. Can you identify the criteria they all have in common?

They all:

◆ Know you.
◆ Like you.
◆ Trust you to take care of their clients as if they were a member of your family.
◆ Reciprocate: They are loyal to you because you are loyal to them.
◆ Refer you over and over – they have a high lifetime value.

Using a Honeypot to Convert Suspects to Prospects

You accept a speaking engagement in front of an audience of 200 people, yet only five or six of them come up to you afterward and ask for additional information.

Your goal is to take advantage of this opportunity and find out exactly who in the room is interested in your services.

Right now, you only *suspect* the people at your speaking engagement will one day convert into some form of business. Some of them will, you just don't know who. You have no idea which of them has an interest in your services.

Much like in a police investigation, we treat everyone as a suspect until we know something different.

You invest your time, money, and energy in connecting with people you *suspect* will be excellent clients if they come to you and ask for help. That's why it is critical you put people into your RaporMax® System.

You've primed the RaporMax® System with people from your natural network. Some of them have referred business to you. Others have called you with interest, and a few may have become clients. As you add more people to the system, from speaking engagements, writing articles, leveraging advertising, social media, networking, and your primary internet presence, you'll notice your phone will ring more often.

Your goal is to convert as many suspects into prospects as possible.

Other than the original members of your natural network – your friends, family, and current business associates – you probably will not know the names and contact information for people you suspect may be great clients. When you show up at a venue full of suspects to deliver a speech, or when you write an article for a trade publication read in an industry full of your ideal clients, or when you place an advertisement targeted at your ideal client, you will need a way to get contact information and gauge level of interest.

That's where the honeypot comes in. It is one of the most important aspects of the 60 Second Sale system. I call it a honeypot because it attracts new prospective clients to you like bees are attracted to a pot of honey.

Instead of standing in front of people and saying, "Call me!" or writing an article and hoping people find you from the byline at the end or offering the sale of a product in an ad, you offer your honeypot in exchange for the contact information of the person in the audience.

Remember the "frat boy" approach? That's old-school sales. The frat boy would get up in front of the audience at a speech and say:

"Here's my product. Buy it!" Instead, we get in front of the audience and ask them to go out on a second date.

Carrying the dating analogy through: The speaking engagement or the published article (or any of the other client attraction systems) is the cup of coffee, and our offer of the honeypot is a request for a second date and a courtship.

Sales has changed. You now need to build a relationship with your prospective client before asking for their money. The honeypot is the next natural step in your prospective client demonstrating interest in who you are and the value you provide (see Figure 5.2).

You can use any information product as a honeypot. The idea is to offer something to your audience that is relevant to the main problem you get paid to solve.

For example: You may have seen the commercials on television for attorneys targeting people who have mesothelioma. This is a rare, particularly deadly form of cancer diagnosed in less than 3,000 people per year in the United States (according to the American Cancer Society). Since mesothelioma occurs primarily as a result of exposure to asbestos in the workplace, and since this connection has been known for decades, an employer who exposes employees to asbestos is clearly negligent.

Plaintiff attorneys who handle mesothelioma exposure cases must be skilled at proving the exposure was preventable, but if they do, a lawsuit will typically result in a large recovery for the injured party (and a significant fee for the attorney).

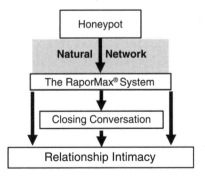

FIGURE 5.2 **A Honeypot Converts Suspects into Prospects**

Attorneys will use a honeypot in their advertising to mesothelioma victims. You will often see commercials on television or ads on the Internet offering a free booklet titled *How to Live with Mesothelioma* or *How to Survive Mesothelioma*. These books contain information about treatment and inspirational stories of survivors. They detail the expenses required to make sure you explore all options. The book also offers you the opportunity to have a free consultation with a law firm that specializes in handling mesothelioma cases.

In this example, the mesothelioma book is a honeypot designed to attract people who have this disease and help the law firm identify those people. It also serves as a tool to motivate the reader to call the law firm (treatment for mesothelioma is expensive and the book points this out). Once people request the book, the law firm now has identified them as prospects.

One additional element of the honeypot that is subtle in this case: the element of expertise. The book is written by an attorney who has worked with hundreds of people stricken with this form of cancer. He is writing from his experience with people who have survived. This makes him an expert on mesothelioma survival. If you have that disease, that's the person you want to talk to.

THREE GOALS IN USING A HONEYPOT

1. *Educate your audience.* Your audience may have some idea that they have a problem, or they may have some goal in the far off distance they want to achieve. You need to help them see just how serious the problem is or just how close they really are to that goal. Put things in perspective for them.

2. *Motivate the audience members to act.* It is never easy to convince someone to act – even if taking action is a way to achieve a goal or avoid pain. You must demonstrate to the audience the consequences of inaction. Will they miss out on something? Will they be overwhelmed by adverse circumstances? How bad can it get?

3. *Position you as the ultimate expert in your field.* Your audience must know the qualifications of a real expert in your field. They must hear the objective criteria that define expertise and then discover how you meet or exceed those criteria.

Types of Engagement Devices You Can Use as a Honeypot

The most common type of honeypot is a white paper or special report. These are easy to develop and can be customized for specific groups, audiences, or on a particular topic. White papers or special reports are ideal for business-to-business audiences.

If your honeypot is lengthier or is for a consumer-focused audience, you may want to make it into a booklet rather than a white paper.

Videos, webinars, and online education courses are powerful honeypots because of the value of the information they contain and the perception of value of educational material. If you would typically charge hundreds of dollars for your educational course and you offer it to your audience as a honeypot for free, it will be a powerful motivator.

Attendance at a live event can also be a highly effective honeypot. You can offer tickets to an event you are conducting as an incentive for a suspect to raise their hand and indicate their interest in your product or service.

For the purposes of our demonstration, we are going to use a special report (in business-to-business sales we call this a *white paper*). The construction of the honeypot in other forms of media is identical.

How to Build the Ideal Honeypot

Here's the outline for creating your honeypot.

Step One: The Opening

Step Two: Frame the problem.

Step Three: Introduce the consequences.

Step Four: Introduce a general solution.

Step Five: Outline qualifications.

Step Six: Describe how you solve these problems.

Step Seven: Issue the call to action.

Step One: The Opening Right from the outset, get people emotionally involved in finding a solution to their problem.

The first step in the honeypot creation process is the opening. You want to pull the readers into the story. You want to get them involved in what's going on in their life and you want to make them feel something.

You're looking to make an emotional connection. The best way to do this is to use a story to draw the reader in. Think of the opening of a really good movie. It grabs you right from the beginning and demands your attention. The opening of your Honeypot must be a story that makes that kind of powerful connection.

The story I tell is the "Wake-Up Call Story" I shared during the introduction to this book. It is the story of how I was rushing down Sixth Avenue in New York City to see a client and I was struck by a taxicab.

The story makes an immediate emotional connection with the reader. Your opening story must be compelling. It can be an experience you've had or it can be a case study from one of your clients. Tell the story in a way that makes a powerful connection. You want the reader to believe that whatever happened in the story could happen to them.

Step Two: Frame the Problem   In this step, you put the problem in perspective for the readers. You get them to be able to clearly identify the problem. Often, people are too close to a situation to see the issue they face. Like a patient in a doctor's office, they often identify symptoms and try to resolve them instead of identifying the actual disease and treating it.

Framing the problem is helping your reader see the disease and recognize they've been focusing on the wrong thing. You do this by highlighting what happened in the story that you've told and pointing out that the main character was focused on one thing but should have been focused on something else.

You don't want to come directly out and hit the reader in the face with the fact that they've been wrong. Let them draw that conclusion from the story you've told. Having the readers realize for themselves that they've been focusing on the wrong thing all this time is a massive breakthrough. If, however, you blatantly point it out, they may get defensive and reject your assertion.

You need to create a bridge between what happened in the story and what's happening to your client. Lead them down the path by the hand but don't accuse them directly of misinterpreting their situation.

Again, the analogy to the doctor is apropos. Imagine that your reader has some sort of disease and it's your job to help her detect the disease by outlining the symptoms but being careful to point out that treating the symptoms don't cure them.

You tell your reader, "This is what you'll notice if you have this problem, 1, 2, 3, 4, 5." You outline the symptoms, like a checklist, enumerating them.

Have you ever watched a documentary or news report on a specific disease? People look directly into the camera and describe their symptoms. What happens to you during the hours after that show ends? Well, for some people, what happens is that they begin to experience some of those symptoms. Nagging headaches, anxiousness, rapid eye twitching, fatigue, loss of appetite, stomach cramps, dry mouth. Do *I* have this disease? They make an appointment and see a doctor. The minute they visit the doctor, however, all those symptoms seem to go away.

Well, we are doing something similar in this white paper, except your reader actually has the problem. You are going to highlight the symptoms to show her the need for action.

Step Three: Introduce the Consequences of Leaving This Problem Unaddressed   The reader will reflexively ask: "What happens if I do nothing?"

The status quo is your biggest enemy. You've got to get moving in the right direction.

Address the "elephant in the room." Talk about why the reader might not take action to solve this problem. That's difficult. Most sales experts will tell you to never put a negative idea in your prospect's mind. My philosophy is different. If your prospective client is thinking about something, I want you to get it out into the open.

When you're creating your white paper, you need to specifically hit home why the status quo is no longer acceptable. That's a huge point. The client has not acted to solve this problem. She must find the motivation within.

You need to share with your readers what will happen to them if they don't solve the problem. Be as specific, be as focused, and be as graphic as possible. For each consequence, you need to list out why it's so bad. Explain the worst-case scenario.

Here's how I do it in my business:

If you don't come up with a system for creating deeper relationships, your financial situation will erode rapidly.

For starters, you will lose a lot of business to your competition. Your attrition rate will soar to 25%, 35%, 45% each year. That means it's more difficult to replace that business, and it costs you almost 50% more to attract new clients. That's a huge increase in your client attraction dollars. It's a huge increase in your sales budget as well as a huge increase in the amount of time you need to spend going out and finding new clients.

A 45% increase in your attrition rate will result in a need to spend more money to attract new clients. If it costs you 45% more to attract new clients, your average client acquisition costs will drive your profit margin into negative territory. That means a loss on each sale. No business can survive that.

Whenever you can tie consequences to a financial outcome, you're making a compelling case. When you present the consequences, you have to help people understand why each consequence is so bad. Readers need to fear the consequences of inaction. That is the key. They have to dread the impending doom of inaction.

That's how you motivate people.

Step Four: Introduce a General Solution   Now it's time to introduce your readers to the solution for their problems. It is not time to tell them to hire you. At least, not yet. But it is time to introduce them to the idea of seeking assistance from someone in your profession or with your solution to their problem.

You begin this section by announcing that there is good news. A solution is available. That general solution announcement could be something as simple as:

- ◆ "Hire a qualified attorney to address this situation." Or
- ◆ "Engage a qualified CPA to help you with your taxes so that you don't have to worry about the consequences of poor tax planning." Or
- ◆ "Prescribe a fast-acting medication to treat your patient."

Just because we are calling this a *general solution,* that doesn't refer to the activities that need to be performed. So although you may write:

♦ "Engage a qualified CPA to help you with your taxes so that you don't have to worry about the consequences of poor tax planning."

You also write:

♦ "Your CPA will also help you avoid audits of your books from any or all of the last seven years."

Also, you should explain why this solution is ideal:

♦ "CPAs are trained professionals; they've seen cases like yours hundreds of times. They can provide you with solutions quickly so that you can put this problem behind you and move on to what you really want to do in your business."

Then explain the likelihood of success:

♦ "A qualified CPA has done this so many times, it's 90% likely they will resolve this issue."

Make sure you reiterate the odds of bad things happening if they don't choose to solve the problem. You have to present the solution and then you'll also have to present the consequences in real numbers.

For example:

♦ "50% of these cases wind up with people going to jail if they don't select the right lawyer." Or "80% of the time, a person who does this without the proper guidance or help fails."

Statistics and probability are valuable tools. Use them and help the reader understand that the odds are not in their favor if they don't select a qualified solution.

Remember that in this section we are talking about a general solution. You're not promoting yourself or your business. You're not the only person qualified to help them solve this problem. If you sell a product, your product is not the only product that can help solve this problem. You may be the best, though, and you want them to realize, on their own, that you're best.

That is the next step in this process.

Step Five: Outline the Qualifications of the Person, the Product, or the Service That Will Solve the Problem This section of the paper is about listing, in as much detail as possible, the qualifications of the ideal professional, service provider, or product to be used as a solution to the problem. Still, you are not making any references to you.

You want to present a preponderance of evidence, and it has to be overwhelming. The qualifications should be similar – in fact, they should be an exact match to your qualifications.

I want you to also be specific and again make it a list. The reader's brain processes a list very effectively. List out the qualifications, bullet point by bullet point. One after the other.

Here are some questions you should answer in this section:

◆ How many years of experience should the ideal service provider have? (How long should the ideal product be on the market?)
◆ What certifications should the ideal service provider possess?
◆ What awards indicate an outstanding professional in this area?
◆ Is there a certain level of experience necessary to master the skills of this profession or solution?
◆ Is there an exclusive or proprietary method, product, or solution available to address this issue?
◆ What differentiates the best in this industry from everyone else?
◆ What criteria are most important when selecting a provider or product to address this issue?

Step Six: Describe Your Services, Your Solution, Your Product, and Your Specific Qualifications The next step in this process is where you list your qualifications. This is a thinly veiled pitch. You are creating a transition in your white paper from an educational document to a document designed to highlight the reasons why you are the ultimate solution for this problem.

You are still not going to say: "Hey, I'm the most qualified. Hire me."

But the evidence will point in your direction, and the client will draw that as a natural conclusion.

The heading of the section should be: "A Little Information about X,Y,Z Company."

In this section, you list each and every single qualification you possess. You list them in the same exact order that you listed the qualifications of the general solution. If, in step 5, you say the reader needs to hire a service provider who has 30 or more years of experience, your first point in step 6, should be, "We have 30 years of experience in this area solving this problem."

For each qualification that you list, you're going to list a case study or you're going to provide a testimonial. In your case study or testimonial, you're going to use the names of real clients, with their permission. You're going to show that you were able to solve their problem by giving the testimonial or at least a quote. It is important to put supporting information with each qualification. This is not the time to be shy.

You don't need to do the talking and say you're the best. You can have your clients do it for you. Put full names of clients, and if you work in the business-to-business space, it should be the full name of the client, his or her position, and his or her company.

Many clients will be happy to do it as long as you discuss it with them in advance. Clients like to be featured in publications. It provides them with recognition and a sense of status.

Step Seven: Issue the Call to Action　The final element of your white paper is a call to action. You need to give your clients specific actionable steps they can take after they read the report.

The minute they put the report down, what should they do? You need to tell them.

Make them a specific offer, give them specific steps to take after reading the report. After you do that, make the consequences of inaction clear. Don't be confusing. Don't offer multiple options. Give them an assignment.

If you want them to call, give them the phone number numerous times (put it on the heading of each page and in the text with the call to action).

If you want them to email, put that down numerous times.

If you want them to go to a website and opt in to receive something, put that down.

But only give them one action, one assignment. Remember to reiterate the consequences of inaction. That's the final punch in the gut, designed to remind clients that they will have this problem forever if they don't take action, right now.

A Word about Your Natural Network and Continuing Communication

The people we targeted in Chapter 3 – the original folks in your natural network – may enter the RaporMax® System without having received a honeypot. If they do, I encourage you to send it to them with one of your initial emails. These folks, presumably, already have a significant level of trust in you because of the relationship you have with them. You can position the honeypot as a valuable report you've authored. Ask them for feedback on it.

Referrals from evangelists will also go directly into the Rapor-Max® System (Figure 5.3). You should also offer them the honeypot information, as a way to introduce yourself and the services you provide. For everyone else, the honeypot is the gateway into your natural network.

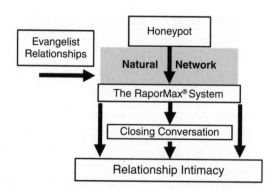

FIGURE 5.3 **Evangelist Relationships Deliver High-Trust Prospects**

60 Second Actions

- ◆ Go through your list of contacts and organize them into groups labeled "prospects," "clients," and "evangelists." This list will now be referred to as your database. Your goal is to grow this database over time by targeting suspects.
- ◆ Immediately get to work on your honeypot so you can use it with the seven systems we outlined in the chapter.
- ◆ Once your honeypot is complete, send it via email to everyone in your natural network.
- ◆ Explore different honeypot topics for the different target audiences you identified during your Ideal Relationship Targeting 21 exercise.

Chapter 6

Put Your Mouth Where the Money Is

60 Second Summary

This chapter will help you start new relationships with large groups of people, in 60 seconds or less. The first minute of your presentation will determine whether people will listen to you. Once they listen, they will want to hear more, and they'll want you to help them.

You will leave the venue with permission to communicate with dozens and often hundreds of people who want to continue the relationship beyond the speech.

What's in This Chapter for You?

You are going to discover a process for structuring a speech for maximum relationship-development impact. This is one of the fastest ways to connect with large numbers of people who will give you permission to communicate with them in the future.

The key concept you will discover in this chapter is the eleven-step process to use speaking engagements as a way to attract new prospective clients. This process is powerful, and it will help you add hundreds of prospects to your database each year.

Being in front of an audience is the most powerful way to enhance your credibility. You will be introduced by someone, every pair of eyes in the room will be on you, and for a period of time, you will be the only one talking. People will ask you questions. People will want more information. You will be considered an authority on the topic of your speech.

This chapter will help you make the most of those opportunities.

One Speech, Two-Dozen Relationships, and a Lifetime of Value

It was a Wednesday afternoon two weeks before Thanksgiving when the email hit my inbox. It was a reply to my weekly email to my database.

Talitha, nicknamed "Tally," an attorney from Los Angeles, had been in my RaporMax® System and reading my emails for a couple of years, and this was the first time she reached out to me. In the message, she told me she and her husband, Bill, were members of a group and they were looking for a speaker for a meeting. She asked if I was interested.

A few moments later, I was on the telephone with Bill, one of the premier litigators in the United States. Bill was running a meeting of a group called the Complex Commercial Litigation Institute, and they were looking for someone to do a class on relationship-based client attraction (lawyers hate the word *sales* and they never use it).

I jumped at the opportunity.

The meeting was in February in Las Vegas, and there were senior executives from 24 law firms in attendance. My role was to provide two educational presentations and hold informal mentor sessions with the attendees, one-on-one, during the course of the three-day meeting.

Since the meeting was by invitation only, I was able to connect with most of the attendees in advance. I sent a physical letter and copies of a couple of my books as a way to introduce myself. I followed this letter with an email survey asking some discovery questions about the individual attorney as well as the challenges facing each attorney's firm.

When I arrived in Las Vegas, I was invited to the welcome reception and the dinner, where I was seated next to Bill and Tally. It wasn't until that moment that I was struck by the risk they were taking. They had bet their reputations on someone they had never met. Bill presented me to this group of polished, successful litigators as an expert on business relationships, without ever having met me in person and after only having a couple of telephone conversations with me. Upon meeting this extraordinarily successful couple, I thanked them for their trust.

That weekend remains one of the most memorable business experiences of my career. I mentored and learned from some of the sharpest minds in the legal profession. They viewed me as a peer in every way – except in business strategy and client attraction; in that aspect they viewed me as an expert.

Success is measured in many ways. That weekend was a huge success because of the door it opened to that organization. It was a success because of the value I provided. It was a success because of the lifetime financial value I continue to realize as a result of that speaking engagement. But most importantly of all, that weekend was a success because of the relationships I developed.

As I was saying goodbye to Bill and Tally at the end of that weekend, Bill thanked me for making him look good. He said I was everything he and Tally had come to know from reading my emails the past couple of years.

Tally found me while searching the internet looking for information about relationship-based sales for lawyers. When she visited my website, she was tempted by the honeypot I posted. I offered all website visitors a free CD with an audio education program. After receiving the CD, I continued to communicate with Tally for years through a weekly email sent out each Wednesday at noon.

While email communication is asynchronous, it has the effect of establishing a relationship between the reader and the writer, much the same way a book does. When people who have read the email over time finally meet the author, they often feel as though they are old friends.

The trust that was established during the email relationship was reinforced when Bill and Tally saw me speak to the audience at the Complex Commercial Litigation Institute session. While that speaking engagement deepened their trust in me, it also helped to begin several other relationships. Speaking in front of an audience is one of the most powerful ways to get new relationships off to a powerful start.

Credibility, Visibility, and Differentiation

Speaking in front of a group of people quickly provides you with three important advantages that would otherwise require years to establish. As someone giving a presentation, talk, or speech, you immediately have the opportunity to establish credibility, gain visibility, and differentiate yourself from everyone else in your field. These three attributes are the building blocks of trust, and there is no faster way to establish them than speaking in front of an audience.

CREDIBILITY

You don't have to be a professional speaker to leverage the power of speaking engagements to start relationships. After graduating from college, I took a job as a bellman with Marriott hotels. I hustled carrying bags, giving directions, and driving guests around Westchester County, New York, for 8 months, when a management position in the housekeeping department opened up.

This was my opportunity. My ambition was to someday be a hotel general manager, and housekeeping was as good a place as any to start. After interviewing for the role, I was awarded the position as a housekeeping manager in training in the same hotel where I was a bellman. On Friday afternoon I was a bellman; the next Monday, two days later, I was a housekeeping manager.

On the first day, when I met with my new boss, the department director, he informed me that each day the manager would hold a "stand-up" meeting with the entire shift of workers in the hallway by the time clock. He told me he wanted me to run the meeting that morning (my first day on the job). He handed me an index card with three topics and some notes.

He said, "Review this for a few minutes before we start. I will introduce you and then you'll cover the three points on this card."

I did what the boss asked and the 30-plus people standing in the hallway around me listened, nodded appropriately, and applauded when I finished. Many of them came up to me and shook my hand, welcomed me, and wished me well.

That time I spent in front of the housekeeping team on my first day, all of about 60 seconds, established my credibility with the group as an authority. By virtue of getting in front of them and sharing valuable information in a competent way, I demonstrated knowledge, confidence, and leadership.

This is called *situational authority* and you have it whenever you speak in front of a group of people.

One of the best ways to describe this is by thinking of a golf pro and a surgeon. When you walk through the doors of a hospital and into an operating room, the surgeon is in charge. He has the talent, skills, knowledge, and experience, and he's honed them over time.

The minute the surgeon steps into the tee box at the country club, he's looking to the golf pro for help with his swing.

Getting up in front of the housekeeping team established my credibility quickly via situational authority and speaking to an audience can do the same for you.

VISIBILITY

Before someone can enter into a relationship with you, they first must know who you are and what you do. Speaking engagements are a fantastic introduction because they offer you tremendous leverage. Instead of introducing yourself to one person and talking about how you can help them, you have the ability to introduce yourself to dozens, hundreds, or even thousands of people.

When you are booked to speak in front of a group, you have an added bonus working for you. Everyone in the audience is there for a common purpose. They all signed up to attend this meeting, they all belong to this particular group, and they all have some connection to its mission. When you become adept at speaking to groups, you'll find that people in the audience will share your contact information with others who share the same affinity, and that will help you gain visibility within the industry. This means your visibility can extend beyond the walls of the room within which you are appearing.

DIFFERENTIATION

The third powerful element speaking engagements offer is differentiation. This is an opportunity to demonstrate what makes you unique and special in your field. When you take to the front of the room, you have the attention of the audience and you can do virtually anything you want with it. Use this time to show the value you provide and draw a distinction between how you provide this value and the way others in your industry perform.

To maximize these three qualities and take advantage of the leverage available from speaking engagements, I've created an 11-step process to help you structure your speech:

1. Seize credibility with an origin story.
2. Deliver powerful information.
3. Entertain the audience.
4. Demonstrate a clear need for the value you provide.
5. Build on emotion with a presentation arc.
6. Include success stories and testimonials.
7. Provide a solution.
8. Highlight the complexity.
9. Offer your honeypot.
10. Provide action-oriented guidance.
11. Collect contact information.

Let's break down each of these steps so you can put together the perfect speech.

Step One: Seize Credibility with an Origin Story

Whenever you are booked to give a speech, you need to send an introduction to the meeting organizer, print the introduction and hand it to the organizer the day of the speech, and insist that it is read exactly as you've written it. Even after you do all that, I can assure you something will go awry.

The Toughest Introduction Ever Back in October 2003, I was out in Kansas City to do a presentation for a home improvement company. This was a 60-store chain that serviced all of the Midwest.

I was the keynote speaker at their annual convention, and the place was jam-packed.

Typically, these events are high-energy gatherings where they give out awards and announce who is going to win salesperson of the year.

Add to that the fact that this particular company was family run with deep roots in the community and you have the making of a really great crowd, which for a speaker is fantastic.

The meeting was in a local theater, and because they were giving out annual awards after my talk, there were salespeople from 60 stores in attendance, with spouses and special invited guests.

In total, we're talking about 1,500 to 2,000 people.

I was waiting off stage for the company's head of sales to introduce me.

He wasn't in the building when I arrived, which was odd, but now, as the time for the speech approached, I noticed him walk into the backstage area, whisper to the guy doing the lighting, and march right past me onto the stage.

People applauded politely, and the lights came up.

He grabbed the microphone from the stand.

"Ladies and gentlemen, we have a special guest here. David Lorenzo is one of the country's foremost experts on business strategy and relationship development. We've flown him in to share some wisdom with us and inspire us.

As I'm sure some of you know, our former CEO was found shot in his home yesterday, and we've received news he passed away just a few minutes ago.

(The crowd groans, murmurs, and shifts uncomfortably in their seats.)

Now, folks … (crowd still stirring)

Now, I know this is a difficult time since this is a family-owned company and this man was like a father to many of us.

(At that point the announcer begins to choke up.)

We are going to cancel the festivities scheduled for later in the day.

But since he's come all this way, please join me in welcoming … Dave Lorenzo."

It has been many, many years since that awkward situation, and I'm giving you permission to laugh. Not because what those folks were going through was funny – far from it. The reason you can laugh is because once you find yourself in that situation as a speaker, you have confidence you can overcome a great deal of adversity.

I took the stage and made a few comments about teamwork and forming a bond during difficult times. After that, I remarked that people probably would want to pay their respects to the family, so I'd be happy to return and give the full speech when the company rescheduled their awards event.

The guy who introduced me was in a grief-driven fog and didn't think to cancel the speech. He was mortified; he called me a couple of weeks later to apologize. I said: "Don't worry. I'm not at all upset. But next time please read the introduction exactly as it was written!"

We both had a great laugh and the company was a valuable client for many years.

The point: Don't rely on the person introducing you to follow your instructions.

After you are introduced, no matter how good or bad, take a moment and introduce yourself. Do this by using an origin story. Your origin story tells the audience who you are, how you got here, and why they should listen to you.

There are many ways to do this, but the easiest way is to just come out and say it. You can use an opening like this:

"Thank you. It is an honor to be here with you today. Whenever I attend an event like this, and a new speaker takes the stage, I often find myself wondering: 'Who is this guy, and why should I listen to him?' In case some of you are asking yourselves those questions, I'd like your permission to spend a moment answering them for you about me. Is that all right?"

Don't wait for an answer. Just say, "Thanks!" and go into your origin story.

STEP TWO: DELIVER POWERFUL INFORMATION

People want action. Think of your favorite movies. Whenever the plot begins to drag, they throw in a car chase. The content portion of your speech should be one car chase scene after another. Move quickly through your points and use lots of lists. Our brains respond well to lists of things. They like order.

Speak quickly when delivering facts and figures and slow down when telling stories.

Move around the stage or the front of the room. When making a critical point, run from one side to the other (do that only once but at an apropos moment). Use your movement to help keep people engaged. Choreograph it and rehearse the timing.

STEP THREE: ENTERTAIN THE AUDIENCE

Along with your movement around the stage, you should also vary your voice inflection. Interrupt your rhythmic cadence frequently by lowering your voice to a whisper for emphasis (always use a microphone when provided) and then raise it to a shout at other times.

Tell stories to support your key points but make sure they are succinct. The best stories come from your personal experience, and they are always easier to remember than stories told to you.

Never, ever, try to get away with passing off another person's story as your own. It is fine to pass along another person's idea, as long as you give people credit. But your credibility will never recover from "borrowing" a story.

Use humor if you are well versed in the art of comedy. Never make an audience member the object of your joke. Never poke fun at your host. Never, ever, use foul or objectionable language in a professional presentation.

The safest subject for your jokes is YOU. Self-deprecation is a useful tool to help win over an audience. Make certain you poke fun at yourself in a way that doesn't damage your credibility. Always use self-deprecating humor in a way that takes it outside the context of the work you are doing.

If you are really serious about adding humor to your talks, I encourage you to write a few jokes and try them at an open mic night at a local comedy club. There is nothing more valuable than the instant feedback you receive from a live audience. Keep trying new jokes until you have a dozen that work for all types of audiences.

STEP FOUR: DEMONSTRATE A CLEAR NEED FOR THE VALUE YOU PROVIDE

Help the audience see and feel the value you have to offer by presenting a case study or a story with high emotional impact. Draw them into the story by demonstrating how "this can happen to you …"

Use actual examples from public records or stories in the public domain. Get permission from clients to share some of their stories.

Show how crazy things happen to smart people in their industry, role, or situation.

Find multiple ways to say: "This can happen to you." Throughout your talk. For example:

- ◆ "Here is a common disastrous mistake ..."
- ◆ "This happened to the industry leader just last year. Don't take anything for granted ..."
- ◆ "Anybody can fall into this trap. This company thought it was doing everything right – until it wasn't. You probably think you're doing everything right, too."
- ◆ "Here's something I want you to watch out for. One of my best clients ignored this advice and got burned ..."

STEP FIVE: BUILD ON EMOTION WITH A PRESENTATION ARC

Like a movie or a feature television program, your presentation should have an arc. In this book, we talk a great deal about clarity of purpose. That means staying focused on why you are doing a particular activity. As you discovered at the beginning of this chapter, your purpose for delivering a speech is to start a relationship with as many people as possible. You want the entire room to come running for your honeypot.

Your presentation arc should support that purpose.

Begin with your origin story and explain why you're qualified to cover this subject. Make an emotional connection with stories. Take the audience to the depths of hell with worst-case-scenario case studies and tales of what can happen if they don't follow THE rules – YOUR rules.

Then give them hope by sharing a client success story. Give them inspiration by providing some testimonials from actual people who know you and have worked with you. Finally, offer them a payoff by sharing a honeypot that will help them select a hero (you) to solve their problem or help them achieve a goal.

STEP SIX: INCLUDE SUCCESS STORIES AND TESTIMONIALS

I alluded to these in step 5. If you have actual clients in the audience, and you've secured their agreement beforehand, invite them onto the stage to deliver a testimonial. You shouldn't prepare what they are going to say. You should simply get agreement from them before the speech and tell them they will have three to five minutes to tell their story.

This will be powerful because it is real.

An alternative or an addition to the testimonial is the full-detail case study. Get client permission to share everything about one of your successful client relationships. Use pictures and even video to enhance the story.

Step Seven: Provide a Solution

While you are breaking down the case study or after you listen to the testimonial, describe what you did that made things work. Help the audience see the action you took, the recommendation you made, or the product you provided. Before and after photos are powerful.

It is really important to show the people in attendance WHAT you did but not HOW you did it. You don't include the HOW for three reasons:

1. That's too involved and you don't have enough time.
2. You may need to modify some actions for each case, and people will pick you apart on the specifics.
3. The people who want to get that deep into the weeds in a presentation setting are probably not going to be great clients because they are likely "do-it-yourself" folks.

Step Eight: Highlight the Complexity

Too often, sales executives and professionals make the solution look too easy. They do this because they want to give the audience a good feeling. They don't want them to be afraid or feel as though the situation is hopeless.

The audience members should only have a good feeling if they hire you. The audience members should only feel hopeful if they agree to work with you. Do not minimize the work you do or the expertise required to do it.

In fact, you should go in the opposite direction. Make sure you tell the audience about the complexity of the process and the education you received through trial and error. Make sure they know about the pitfalls of "going it alone." Make sure they understand that the status quo will be disastrous and action is necessary.

Make it a point to demonstrate how you cut through all that complexity and make it LOOK easy.

Envision a heart surgeon. He's performed hundreds of surgeries. He can do most catheterization procedures blindfolded. But if he described that specific procedure to you, your head would spin.

Show them how you make the complex look simple.

STEP NINE: OFFER YOUR HONEYPOT

You cannot cover any subject in a comprehensive way during a speech. You are there only to pique their interest and get permission to follow up. That's why you've developed your honeypot. This is the point in the presentation where you offer it to the audience.

When your speech is 75% complete, right before you take questions – if you choose to do so – you stop what you are doing and say:

> "You know, I almost forgot. This subject is so detailed, I've prepared a special report to address some of the points I won't be able to cover during our time together today. The title of that report is '<Title>'. If you'd like a free copy of this report, pass your business cards to the center aisle and I will pick them up at the end of our time together."

You will collect these cards at the end of your talk.

Do not skip this step. This is the entire reason you are there – to add people who are interested in your services to your RaporMax® System.

STEP TEN: PROVIDE ACTION-ORIENTED GUIDANCE

You must tell your audience what to do when the talk is over. Some people will have questions, and they will want to rush the stage and ask you. Some will just want to congratulate you on a great talk. Almost all of them will want your honeypot. And one or two may want to talk about hiring you or buying your product or service.

Keep your clarity of purpose and tell them to pass their business cards to the center aisle and you'll come around and collect them.

Ask them to follow you to the back of the room and meet you there and, after you have all the business cards, you'll be happy to answer questions.

Be specific and focused.

Basking in the glory of a great speech is a great way to miss out on follow-up opportunities.

STEP ELEVEN: COLLECT CONTACT INFORMATION

At the end of your talk, say, "Thank you," and before the applause stops move quickly down the center aisle and pick up all the business cards people have passed over. When you get to the end of the aisle, stand by the exit door and collect more cards.

Don't stop to answer questions. If people stand in front of you to ask questions while you are standing by the back door, move them to one side, so you can keep making eye contact with people leaving and keep collecting business cards.

Don't forget: This is the entire reason you are giving a speech – to attract people who are interested in your services and add them to your RaporMax® System (see Figure 6.1).

Collect every business card people want to give you. Don't take questions. Don't take extended bows on stage. Don't wait for people to stop clapping.

Get the contact info. Got it?

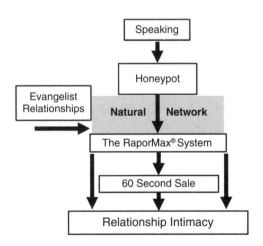

FIGURE 6.1   **Speaking Engagements Attract Engaged Prospects**

That is the step-by-step guide I've been using for leveraging speaking engagements to build my database for over 20 years. Stay focused on your purpose for taking the stage and you'll always come away with several future clients.

How to Handle Questions

Never take questions at the end of your talk. If you feel the need to take questions, do so when the speech is 75% complete. Say this:

"We have time for just three quick questions. If you have something to ask that you believe will benefit the group, please raise your hand now."

When someone asks a question, repeat what was asked, respond, and then review the entire thing. If, by chance, you get a hostile question, repeat it and respond and then move on – physically and verbally. Don't review. Walk to the opposite end of the stage.

Never, ever, take questions at the end of your talk because it screws up the entire plan. Remember your purpose. Remember why you are there: to initiate new relationships.

How to Attract Speaking Engagements

First: Embrace your speaking celebrity. The most important aspect of getting speaking engagements is offering your services as a speaker to people, associations, and companies. Everyone needs to know about the value you can provide in this area.

Create your own personal website with a domain that matches your name. It doesn't matter if you are a pharmaceutical sales representative or a sales executive for a natural gas company. Create a website and post videos of you speaking to groups of people. Also create a YouTube channel and post videos of you giving tips in your area of expertise. Post speaking videos there as well. These two places are where you are going to direct people who want to book you for a speaking engagement.

Next: Pick one or two topics and own them. Don't offer speeches on leadership, sales, strategy, productivity improvement, work-life balance, truck repair, little league baseball coaching techniques, and how to be a great parent. You may be an expert on all of these things, but people won't know what to book you to speak about.

It is better to pick a narrow niche within your industry and offer deep substantive talks in that area. After six months to a year of delivering talks on specific subjects to the narrow niche market, everyone will be discussing you as an up-and-coming speaker.

Then: Ask your best clients to invite you to their office to deliver your talk. You can do this as an educational talk during a learn-at-lunch event or you could give a speech at their all-employee meeting. The key is to cover a topic in your area of expertise in a way that provides value to them.

Finally: After the client sees you speak live, ask for names of other people within the industry who might benefit from having you over to deliver your talk. Also, ask for names of people they know in industry trade associations.

Those first few actions will help you get your feet wet as a speaker. After you get that experience under your belt, try some of the following options:

- Once each month send an email to your database reminding them about your ability to educate, entertain, and motivate their team. Also let them know you are available for industry events. Always include a link to a video of you speaking to an audience.
- Call the local event venues and see if they can send you lists of conventions and meetings coming to town. Go through that list and offer your services to groups in your industry. Explain that you are local and will not require travel reimbursement.
- Develop your own educational events and invite suspects, prospects, clients, and evangelists to attend. Host these events once or twice each year and spend three to six months promoting them. These events are like relationship accelerators. They fast-forward the recognition of value people have for you, your products, and your services.

Be Clear on Your Purpose

Your focus on developing presentation skills and crafting your content should be solely on initiating new relationships through delivering value. You are a teacher, an entertainer, and a conduit for innovation, but you have only one purpose in going somewhere and standing in front of an audience: Initiate new relationships.

You must be completely committed to "selling" yourself to the audience within the first 60 seconds.

Set your ego aside and forget the standing ovation or the motivational music. Hit the audience right in the mouth with fantastic, valuable, actionable information and then offer to continue to do so afterward.

60 Second Actions

- ◆ Outline a great presentation that will be of value to an audience you've targeted using your Ideal Relationship Targeting 21 question interview.
- ◆ Pitch your presentation topic to presidents of groups and organizations and event planners.
- ◆ Restructure your next set of talks to include the system as outlined in this chapter.
- ◆ Offer your honeypot.
- ◆ Collect contact information from as many people as possible and add them to your RaporMax® System.

Chapter 7

Premier Positioning through Publishing

60 Second Summary

The first 60 seconds someone spends reading an article you've written is critical. This chapter will help you capture the attention of your reader and leverage that attention to start a relationship.

The first 60 seconds an editor spends reading your article pitch will determine if your article is published. This chapter provides you with a template for pitching articles.

Here is your step-by-step guide to increasing visibility, building credibility, and differentiating yourself and your business through publishing.

What's in This Chapter for You?

This chapter will help you develop a body of work that will clearly demonstrate your expertise in your field. If you want to differentiate yourself from everyone else who does what you do, building a cache of published work with intellectual rigor is the best way to do it.

The key concept you will discover in this chapter is the five-step guide to creating an article that will help you attract new prospects. It contains an exact script you can use in email and letters to submit your work.

When clients and prospective clients read the articles you write, they will position you as a leader in your industry. Sharing your ideas with decision makers will help you shape their thought processes.

Your personal brand will be that of an expert beyond the rank and file sales professional. You'll not only stand out from the crowd – you will become a "category of one." By publishing in your field of expertise, you set yourself apart as someone who owns a niche. It is impossible for you to be "just another salesperson."

Publish and Smell the Money

As I walked into the office of a shareholder of one of the largest law firms in the United States, I could almost smell the money. All right, it might have been furniture polish on the mahogany that lined the walls or the leather sofa and armchairs that smelled rich. Regardless, this particular sales call was definitely with a qualified prospect, and he wasted no time at getting to the point:

> I need to develop more business. My partners are giving me a hard time. I've always been successful because I'm a great litigator, and throughout the years I've teamed up with rainmakers who would bring in the cases and turn them over to me. My recent rainmaking partner just became the state's attorney general, so I need to bring some business in the door. I read your book. I agree with your approach. How soon can we get started?

With that, he reached for his checkbook, placed a six-figure check on the table, and extended his hand to shake mine.

"Thanks for agreeing to take me on as a client; I was expecting to pay a lot more," he said with just the right corner of his mouth turning up in a half-smile.

The book to which this gentleman was referring was one I had written in 2012, *Client Attraction Secrets for Lawyers,* published by James Publishing. That book targeted a narrow niche audience, as evidenced by the title, but everyone who calls me after reading it is ready, willing, and able to work with me.

That is the power of publishing. It offers you the holy trinity of sales: visibility, credibility, and differentiation. When people read something you've written, they get a window into your thinking. This accelerates your relationship with them.

The way you write is the way you think. Sharing your thinking helps generate interest in you and your work.

I differentiate writing from publishing because you can write and send your thoughts to people in an email (which I highly encourage you to do with your RaporMax® System) or on your own website. Publishing is when someone else – a credible third party – disseminates your writing.

These publication vehicles are always in need of content. When you complete your Ideal Relationship Targeting 21 interviews, you will have a list of many publications your ideal clients read. These are the places you want to have your articles published. These include:

◆ Online publications for businesses and special interest groups
◆ Printed and electronic newsletters
◆ News websites
◆ Printed and electronic books

Each of these have utility for attracting new prospects.

Online publications always need content. If your ideal clients consume information from a specific website, you should regularly pitch the publisher on your articles. Having an article published there one time is excellent for credibility, but having your articles appear frequently is even better. (Remember, frequency of communication helps to build trust.)

Newspapers and online news websites will often accept content from people who are perceived to be experts in specific areas. The best way to establish yourself as an expert is to start by helping reporters and editors with background information on stories. Here's how you can do that.

Begin by reading the columns in your target paper, on the website, or in the magazine on a regular basis. Identify the reporters who cover the subject matter you want to write about. When a news story breaks on that subject, quickly write up some "talking points" or ideas for stories. These ideas should be just enough to get the reporter interested. After each idea, make sure you include how you can help develop the story for them. Include your bio and contact information.

This makes you an expert in their eyes, and they may call and ask you questions so they can knowledgeably write the story. Eventually, when you've built up enough trust with them, they may quote you in a story. After that happens, you can ask for an opportunity to submit an article to the publication.

Some publications – particularly trade publications – will not have specific reporters on staff. They may rely on freelance journalists to write articles. In this case, your approach should be similar. Instead of pitching the reporter on your areas of expertise, you pitch the editor or publisher directly on article ideas. You can even write up a specific article and send it directly to the editor.

Newspapers and news websites almost always have dedicated reporters covering different areas of the community or different business industries. Their contact information is readily available online, and you can offer your expertise for "background information" on subjects they are currently covering. It is difficult to submit an article for publication to a newspaper, but you can definitely be quoted by a reporter or serve as a source when there is a need for expertise.

It is challenging to have a book published by a traditional publisher. Your idea must be unique, you must be a credible expert, and you must have a platform to help sell books. That last part is most important. Since you have a job and it is not being a full-time author and bookseller, you might not want to go down the road of pitching to book publishers. That's why self-publishing makes sense. Your goal in self-publishing a book is to use it as a tool to open doors for you and to prime people for working with you. The idea: Anyone who reads the book is ready, willing, and able to do business with you.

Five Steps to Attracting New Prospects through Publishing

STEP ONE: WRITE AN ARTICLE PEOPLE WILL SHARE

Wherever you sit down to write a business article, your goal is to motivate the reader to take action. One of those actions is to share the information. To make this happen, you have to evoke emotion within the reader. Here is a writing formula to help you create an article people will want to share:

- ◆ *Headline:* The headline of the article has to be compelling. It has to make the reader sit up and take notice. It should speak directly to the problem the reader is facing, and it should offer some kind of promise.

Look at the headline of this section: "Five Steps to Attracting New Prospects through Publishing."

- The problem: How to attract new prospects.
- The promise: These five steps will help you attract them.
- Address the problem with a promise.

◆ *Opening story:* This is how you connect with emotion. Tell a compelling story. Get the reader to put himself in the place of the main character. When the reader is "in the character's shoes," he will feel what the main character feels. That's what you are looking to achieve.

◆ *Action, guidance, or list:* This is the section where you tell the readers what to do. Give advice here. You can't get into detail – you don't have enough room – but you have to give them something valuable.

◆ *Lesson learned:* Don't be coy. You're not creating the end of *The Sopranos*. People shouldn't guess what the article means. Tell them the lesson they just learned.

◆ *Call to action:* Offer your honeypot. This is where you get them to call you, email you, opt in on a website to get your honeypot. That's the entire point of writing the article, so don't leave this out. Any article you write without a call to action is a waste of time (see Figure 7.1).

Step Two: Send the Article to Trade and Community Publications

If you work in the business-to-business space, trade publications are an ideal venue for you to use to publish your article. When you do your Ideal Relationship Targeting 21 interview, your clients will give you the names of trade publications they read. Ask them for copies. If the publications are online, do the Google dance and search for them.

Every publication has a *masthead*, which is a page that lists everyone who works to get the information together. Find the person with the title "acquisition editor" or "editorial director." Email your article to that person. Also print out a copy and drop it in the mail. Include your bio.

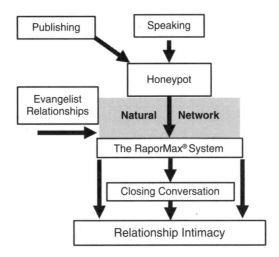

Figure 7.1 **Publishing Produces Prospects**

You should write a cover email and letter and include them with the articles. Here is what the letter and email should say:

Dear Mrs. Smith,

Enclosed, please find an article on <subject>. Each month I write several of these articles; I am happy to provide you with this content at no cost and I give you permission to publish it. I ask that you leave the final paragraph with my contact information intact, so readers may reach out to me for additional information.

If you find this article valuable and you'd like additional content, I am happy to provide it as frequently as necessary.

To discuss this arrangement or for author verification, you may contact me at <your phone number>.

Warm regards,
<Your Name>

You can send the same article to multiple publications. The only time you need to provide exclusive content to a trade publication is when you have a contract to do so.

If you sell to consumers, you should still have a list of publications you've uncovered from your Ideal Relationship Targeting 21 interview. Included in this list will be magazines, newspapers, or websites focused on the local community. There are publications for people looking to hire vendors for the home, community-focused publications, local civic publications, and religious congregation publications. Offer your content to all of them.

Step Three: Follow Up Forever

Publishing is all about persistence. Eventually, the editor will need an article and your email or letter will come at exactly the right time. Don't give up. Keep sending the articles each month until they run them (or tell you to go away).

Editors are busy. Call the editor once after sending your initial email. Leave a message saying you want to make sure they are the correct person to send the article to. Tell them you will send an article each month unless you hear back from them.

Every few months, you can call and leave another message. If you do happen to get an editor on the phone and she tells you they don't accept unsolicited articles, explain that now that you've had a conversation, they know you. Then ask for the editor to request your articles. I know that sounds stupid, but it is stupid for an editor to reject an article with that excuse – yet I hear it all the time.

When I first started sending articles to trade publications, I reached out to a newsletter for lawyers published by a bar association in a big state. I sent articles each month. The editor returned my call almost immediately the first month.

"We don't accept unsolicited articles," he said.

"Fine," I replied. "Now that we've had a conversation, you know me. Can you invite me to send you articles each month? If you hate them, don't run them."

"Sure, whatever," was the less-than-enthusiastic response I received.

I modified my pitch email and letter to make the opening line:

"Thank you for the invitation to submit an article for your publication."

Eventually, that editor was in a bind and needed a great article. He selected one of mine. The reader feedback was excellent. My "column" ran in that publication every month for almost three years. I received a few leads each month, and several of those became clients.

STEP FOUR: PROVIDE YOUR ARTICLE TO SECONDARY PUBLICATIONS

You want people to see you everywhere they turn. You want them asking each other about you. If your article is in a national trade publication, a community newspaper, and on a church website, people will begin to think you are the preeminent expert in your field. That's the idea.

The primary goal is to be published in a trade periodical or other publication your ideal client reads, but while you are making that happen (or after you make that happen), publishing your content in other venues is a smart practice.

One of my clients received an order for a $17 million aircraft as a result of an article he wrote on luxury travel in a community newspaper. The buyer – an aircraft fleet manager for a Fortune 50 company – was waiting to get a haircut in a barbershop and the community newspaper was the only reading material available. The fleet manager read the article, requested the honeypot, and a relationship began.

Secondary publications will almost always gladly accept your content, but you may have to make a few minor modifications to suit their readership. As long as the modifications don't take longer than writing an original article, it's worthwhile. Of course, the offer of the honeypot must remain or the entire exercise is worthless.

A note about church or religious publications: Most people do not explore this publishing avenue, and it is a big mistake. Go to your pastor, rabbi, imam, or clergy leader and explain the value of providing good information to the congregation in areas that go beyond religion. People who worship in your religious institution have lives and interests that go beyond what they receive in the religious services. Providing an entertaining and educational publication (online, physical, or both) is a valuable way to keep the congregation engaged.

Offer to be the editorial director for your place of worship. You can curate articles from other businesses and civic leaders in town. This is yet another way to develop great relationships and have your articles reach more people each month.

Step Five: Rethink, Reuse, and Repurpose

Some of your articles will be better than others. If you submit an article and it receives no reaction – meaning nobody calls you, nobody requests your honeypot, and you are not asked to write another article for that publication – you need to rethink the topic.

In rethinking an article, check with your clients to see if this is still a subject that is of interest to them. If it is, your approach was probably wrong. Take a more controversial stand. Stake out a position that is contrary to what other experts advocate. This will help make an emotional connection with some readers. Don't be afraid of a little disagreement. It's good for business. People who disagree keep reading and, eventually, will look for a point of commonality – it's human nature.

When you have an article that works – that is, people request your honeypot, the editor receives positive feedback, and you're invited to submit additional articles – use that article again with a different publication. As long as neither publication (the place where it first ran or the second publication) requires original content, you're free to run the article again in another place. And you should.

A great article can also make an outstanding story for a presentation or a terrific educational video or even a webinar topic. When you have a subject that is clearly a winner – as verified by your publishing success – repurpose it in other forms of media. If it resonated with your audience once, it will resonate with them again in another venue.

Advanced Publishing Strategy

Our focus has been on publishing articles in media your ideal clients read. This is one of the best ways to direct clients to your honeypot and have them opt in to your RaporMax® System (see Figure 7.1). As you write articles, have them published, and become recognized as an expert in your field, people will ask you to write more often. This is when you may want to consider writing a book or a booklet.

Self-publishing is easier than it has been since Johannes Gutenberg invented the printing press in 1439. There are many services that will take your content and do all the heavy lifting of publishing for you. You can sell your book online and make money to offset some of the costs. You can give your book away to enhance your credibility and attract speaking engagements. If you use a print-on-demand publishing house, you don't need to have the expense of storing inventory and your physical books can cost less than $10 each to produce.

The content for your self-published work can come from your weekly newsletters, articles you've written for publication, or a combination. If your articles average 500 words, you will probably need about 50 to 75 articles with between 5 and 10 common themes for a coherent book.

If you'd like to polish the content and create continuity, you can hire an editor through one of the freelance recruiting services online. There is a good deal of publishing talent available at reasonable rates, and this is an excellent investment.

As a successful sales professional, entrepreneur, or business leader, a published book can help separate you from the crowd. If you have the content and the financial resources, this is an option you should explore.

60 Second Actions

- ◆ Make a list of at least 20 publications to target for article submission, based on your IRT 21 interview results.
- ◆ Write one article using the template in this chapter.
- ◆ Pitch the article using the email and letter templates outlined in this chapter.
- ◆ Repeat this process each month.

Chapter 8

A Place for Your Stuff: Primary Internet Presence

60 Second Summary

Before any appointment you ever have, you must assume the prospect will do an internet search on you. What will come up? This chapter will help you control that.

People who might want to refer you will want to know if you've ever worked with a specific type of client. They won't want to raise your expectations by asking you. Where can they go to learn more about you and what you've done? This chapter puts that issue to rest.

The CEO of a large company can't sleep and is searching the internet for a solution to an esoteric yet pressing problem. You have that solution. How will he ever know? This chapter will drive that CEO to your doorstep.

What's in This Chapter for You?

This chapter will help you develop a media outlet that you control. It will enable you to showcase your brilliance 24 hours per day, seven days per week.

The key concept you will discover in this chapter is the guide to each element of your primary internet presence. When you follow this template, your website will have everything necessary to present you to the world as an expert.

If you want to control your future, consuming the information in this chapter is essential. With a small investment of your time and money, you can create a platform that will educate, entertain, and attract new clients forever.

If you own a business, this chapter will help you discover the value in your own primary internet presence.

If you work for a big company, this chapter will demonstrate that your future is too important to leave in the hands of someone else. You must set up your primary web presence immediately.

If you are a professional, this chapter will help you realize your advanced education was worthless without a way to showcase your brilliance. Your primary web presence is the most logical starting point.

You Need a Website

Imagine you could highlight everything you've ever done and have it ready to display to anyone who wanted to buy from you. Imagine if it was available 24 hours per day, seven days per week. At any time people can explore your thinking on any subject. You could showcase your best ideas.

That is the true purpose of a website, and everyone should have one.

Differentiating yourself as a sales professional, or a business leader, or as an entrepreneur these days is easy. Before every appointment, the person with whom you are meeting is going to do a basic Internet search on you.

It doesn't matter if you are selling auto parts, private jets, pharmaceutical products, real estate, or anything else. They want to know who you are, what you've done, and if you're worthy of the time they've committed to meeting with you.

This is especially important if you work for a big company or represent a well-known brand. People do business with other people. Help them see who you are and, more importantly, how you think.

The way you write is the way you think. You've heard me say that when we discussed the RaporMax® System. You also heard me say that when we discussed publishing. Well, it is just as important on your website.

Primary Internet Presence

These days there are dozens of social media websites to help you connect and establish and deepen relationships with prospects, clients, and evangelists. There are social media tools you should use frequently, but you should always have your own personal website. I call that your *primary internet presence*.

Think of your primary internet presence as your house and social media as different vehicles you drive. You may have a Rolls Royce, a Ferrari, a Bentley, and a jacked-up monster truck, but at the end of every trip, you drive them to your house and park those fancy vehicles in your garage.

The house is your website – your primary internet presence – and the cars are all the flashy social media websites. Everything brings you home eventually. Home is where you live.

As the great comedian George Carlin riffed in one of his most famous sets: You need a place for your stuff. That place is your primary internet presence.

What does this place for your stuff look like?

First: It must have your name on the door. That means the domain must be recognizable as you. I use DaveLorenzo.com, but I also have DLorenzo.com and TheDaveLorenzo.com and DavidVLorenzo.com All of those domains take you to my primary internet presence.

Registering a domain is easy and relatively inexpensive. You may be tempted to get something flashy or cute, but focus on your name or some form of your name, because you want it to be easily identified with you.

Remember, this website will be with you throughout your entire career. Today you are selling widgets for Acme. Tomorrow you may be selling real estate, and 10 years from now you will own your own company, manufacturing widgets and investing in real estate, but you'll still be adding content to your primary internet presence and people will want to see your growth as a sales professional and business leader. They want to check you out, so give them as much information as possible.

CONTENT IS KING

The way the website looks is nowhere near as important as the information on the site. The website should look professional and it should look modern. In fact, just like you'd update your home every few years, you should refresh your personal website too and update it to make it look like you are on top of your game.

There are four types of content you need to have on your primary internet presence:

- ◆ Articles
- ◆ Video
- ◆ Photos
- ◆ Audio

Each of these types of content offers you unique opportunities to engage people who visit and want to explore your thinking.

ARTICLES

This is the most important form of content on your website. Remember the dead horse I keep beating: The way you write is the way you think. These are your thoughts. They took time to put in writing. All kinds of things can come out of your mouth when you are speaking to someone, but composing your thoughts and posting them on a website requires thought and effort.

Make sure you have a specific place on your website to post your articles and make sure they can be sorted by category. You should add all of your weekly newsletters to your website. You should also add any nonexclusive articles you've written.

Search engine optimization is a distant second to sharing your thoughts with the people who want to get to know you. SEO is a massive industry in the United States and elsewhere, and the people in it want you to believe you can manipulate search engine results. Maybe you can, maybe you can't, or maybe everything can change with a shift in an algorithm. We all have an interest in making sure the search engines can deliver the best relevant content to people who need it. Right now, the written word is the most important aspect in a search engine's ability to index your website. Write a lot. Post it on your website.

By the way, I work with a search engine optimization company to make sure my website is always on the good side of the rules. I don't spend a lot of time thinking about keywords or ways to manipulate rankings. I focus on having a clean website with good code that loads quickly and is doing everything the way the search engine bots like to see it.

On content: When in doubt, write it out. You'll never go wrong posting another article.

VIDEO

Just like writing is critical to showcasing your thinking, video is critical to making an emotional connection. Put as much video on your website as you possibly can. Remember to do three important things with your videos:

1. *Categorize them with your written content.* Then people searching for a topic will get a mix of video and articles. They will consume all of it.

2. *Transcribe all videos and post the transcript in the same article right below the video*. This can be a raw transcript. You don't have to make it pretty. The key is to help the search engines understand your content and also to help hearing impaired people connect with your video.

3. *Always save a copy of any video you upload to a service*. Use whatever video-hosting service you like to embed your videos in your website but always save a copy of your original, either on a local drive as a backup or in the cloud. You never know when the video-hosting service you love will disappear, merge, or simply decide they don't love you anymore.

There are a number of ways to shoot and edit video, but the quality of the content is much more important than the quality of the video. Don't get me wrong – you can't look like a homeless person on a three-day crack binge – but you should be yourself. You should speak like a normal human. And you shouldn't spend an enormous amount of time editing your videos.

To get started, push record on an HD camera or on your phone, start talking, and edit out your finger pushing the button to start and stop. It's as simple as that.

Use your topic calendar in your RaporMax® System as a guide to video content. It will help you stay on track.

Photos

Every article must have a photo. People are attracted to things that are visually appealing. Use photos you take yourself. If you must use professional photos, subscribe to a stock photo service. Don't use photos posted by someone else on the internet – that's copyright infringement, it is unethical, and if you get caught, it will cost you money.

I like the Oprah approach. In her magazine, Oprah is always on the cover. Why? Because it's her magazine. Have people take photos of you at different times and in different locations and use them.

Also, take photos of your clients and use them (with their permission). People love seeing images of themselves.

Remember that your website is an additional way to develop and deepen relationships with people. It is perfectly fine to include photos of family and friends. Keep in mind that you want to make sure you are putting your best foot forward, so the photo of you in a bathing suit contest on vacation is probably not a good idea.

AUDIO

Many people like to include audio interviews on their websites. This is an excellent way to provide great content for people who want to learn more about you. If you can attract talented people and interview them, and you have time for this type of commitment, I recommend doing it.

Just like with video, you always want to include a transcript with every audio program you post on your website. The words are necessary to help people search through your website for content they want to review.

Frank Rodriguez: Website Case Study

Frank is a commercial real estate broker. He focuses on selling hotels. One of his clients buys distressed hotels, fixes them up, and converts them into one of the most successful hotel brands in the world. He incorporates website content into the day-to-day activities of his business. Here's how he does it.

Frank has three hotels he is reviewing with his client. The first step is a financial statement review. Frank sends the financial statements to his client and receives feedback.

Frank writes an article for his website about the importance of the financial review in purchasing a distressed real estate property. He details criteria investors should use when making decisions.

Next, Frank visits the three properties with his client. They take pictures and the client shares thoughts on ways to add value to each property.

Frank posts the photos on his website and writes an article on the hidden value in distressed properties.

The client selects one of the three properties and makes an offer. Frank interviews the client on video and finds out the reason why he selected this property and what his plans are for upgrading it. After the deal is closed, Frank posts the video and transcript on his website. The video is outstanding educational content on how to select a distressed property and how to make an offer that is accepted.

During the next 18 months, Frank visits the property, takes photos, and writes articles on everything happening to increase the value. Everything gets posted on his website.

After the property is reflagged, Frank does a recap of the entire process from beginning to end. He interviews the owner for an hour and posts the audio on his website.

During this process, Frank has used his activity as an opportunity to create great content. He's sent many of these articles out to his network in the form of his weekly email newsletter and monthly print newsletter but he's also posted them on his personal website – his primary internet presence. (He's done everything with the client's permission. Anytime you interview someone or post information about them or their business, you need permission.)

As Frank looks to expand his client portfolio, he can send links to the articles he's written to new prospective clients. When they review his body of work with distressed hotels, the prospects will see he is clearly an expert in this area. He has compiled more information derived from experience than anyone else in real estate.

Think about that for a moment. You've pulled off some amazing deals in your career. These deals required you to educate yourself on your clients' businesses. That information is currently stored in your brain (until you forget it). Future clients cannot access it to see how brilliant you are. Give them access by writing articles and posting photos, video, and audio on your website.

TECHNICAL DETAILS

Every time I discuss primary internet presence with a client, I get a boatload of technical questions because people are intimidated by the process of web design, coding, search analytics, and hosting. There are dozens, if not hundreds, of things to think about related to this, and none of them is worth your time. The technical details of your website should not take up one minute you could spend selling. So here is the least you need to know to get your primary internet presence up and running.

Look at your clients' websites. Find one you like. Ask your client for a referral to the people who set up the website. You can pick a template website and have it customized for your purposes. There's nothing wrong with doing that, and it will save you money. The most important thing is the content management system. Select an open source system (a system with code any competent web designer can change). This is where you will post your articles, video, photos, and audio.

You need the following pages on your website:

- *Articles:* This section may also be called a "blog," which is short for "weblog." Let me emphasize, this is the most important aspect of your primary web presence and you need to have it set up for ease of use. The platform, called a content management system, must be user-friendly because you're going to be posting things on it a few times a week. Although I've titled this page "articles," you can call it "content" or you can call it "my thoughts," but it will be the place where you put all the media you create.

- *About page:* This is the page where you post your bio (bio is short for biographical sketch). It is a narrative about who you are, the value you provide, and who you help. This isn't a resume. It's a story. It's *your* story. Make it compelling and write it so people will want to learn more about you.

- *Contact page:* This is a page where you have your address, telephone number, email address, and any other relevant contact info. Some people also have a form that visitors can fill out that is emailed directly to them. The form is fine, but do not omit the other information. Display it prominently. A note about your phone number: Put in in the header so it is displayed on the top of every page. Don't make visitors search for a direct way to reach you.

- *Home page:* Typically, the page your url (web address) points to is a home page. Do not stress out over the content on this page. The information on the page should have one purpose: Help the website visitor find what they are looking for.

Home Page Choices

Your home page should have a few photos – preferably, you with happy clients – and it should offer your visitors a few choices.

- *Home page choice one:* Content (they click on that link to go to the section with all the educational info you've created).
- *Home page choice two:* Find out more about you and contact you (but remember, your phone number is in the header on every page).
- *Home page choice three:* Get your honeypot. This choice should be as a form where you make an offer – a five-sentence "pitch" to the website visitor to get your honeypot. They enter their name and contact info and the honeypot is automatically emailed to them. Plus they're signed up to your email system so they receive your weekly newsletter. After readers opt in to receive this information, you should also immediately call them and send them a personal email.

This third choice – offering your honeypot – should be a part of the template of every page of your website. It should be posted at the bottom of every article. You must offer visitors an opportunity to go right into your RaporMax® System. Your web designer can help set this up (see Figure 8.1).

PLUMBING – BEHIND THE SCENES

Your primary internet presence cannot go down. Nothing will hurt your credibility more than someone putting in your web address and

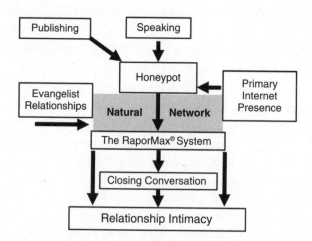

FIGURE **8.1** **Primary Internet Presence Builds Visibility and Credibility**

having it display a message that the site is down. In addition, your website must display quickly. People cannot get a spinning beach ball or some other delay symbol when they enter your domain name. Use a reliable host for your website. Pick a service like Amazon Web Hosting or another reputable service with redundant servers. Also, contract with a company to monitor your website and give them permission to make adjustments if it has any issues. This doesn't cost a lot of money and it will save you headaches.

Do not complicate this process. If you have a limited budget, pick a template website with a predesigned blog, secure your name as the domain, and use that. It will cost you less than $500 to set up (with everything I've outlined here) and less than $20 per month to maintain. One new relationship will return this investment to you.

Even if you have a website for a business you own, you still need this primary internet presence.

Even if you work for a big company, you still need a primary internet presence.

Even if you are a professional – especially if you are a professional – you need a primary internet presence. As an attorney, CPA, architect, financial advisor, real estate agent, or anyone else who sells advice and expertise, you must differentiate yourself from your competition. Providing educational information and entertaining content that helps people get to know you is the way to do this.

Professionals in big firms are particularly deaf to this message. Someday you will not be at a big firm. Someday you will want to be able to attract clients on your own. You need to build a body of work, and you need to have a place to showcase it. Don't hide behind ethics rules. You can write articles and post great content in a way that is compliant, educational, and entertaining.

There are two perfect times to set up your primary internet presence. The first was the day you started your career. The second is right now.

60 Second Actions

- ◆ Search for your name as a domain. Purchase it.
- ◆ Select a web designer and get your primary internet presence up and running ASAP.

- Make sure your phone number is in the website header.
- Put an opt-in box on each page so people can get your honeypot directly from the website.
- Add content to your primary internet presence at least twice each week. This includes articles you send to clients as part of your weekly newsletter.

Chapter 9

Anti-Social Media

60 Second Summary

You want to know which social media platforms make the most sense for you to use to position yourself. This chapter has everything you need to know.

You cannot ignore social media but you also cannot invest all of your time with it because it can be a black hole. I don't deal with "maybe" when it comes to sales. I focus on giving you "sure things."

This chapter delivers the straight scoop on social media for sales superstars.

What's in This Chapter for You?

You'll discover why YouTube is essential and how you can leverage it to attract new prospects in droves.

You will also find out how to use LinkedIn for research and to target your best business prospects.

I try to dissuade you from investing time on Facebook or Twitter unless you have unlimited time and an advertising budget. But I share the one Facebook tool you should keep an eye on.

We also discuss who should use Instagram and who should not, and why.

The key concept you will discover in this chapter is why you should never get into an argument with someone on social media. You can be controversial. You can take contrarian positions. But you shouldn't intentionally single people out and argue with them. This one concept will help keep you from losing lots of business and allow you to maintain your professional reputation.

Don't jump on social media until you read this chapter.

Is This How We Make Friends Now?

During the late summer 2007 I began experimenting with social media as a tool for relationship development. I had a LinkedIn profile since 2005 but I wasn't using it for relationship development purposes. In 2007, I started connecting with interesting people on Facebook and Twitter.

While the growth of social platforms in general increased at a dramatic rate, my use of Facebook and Twitter was heavy but the growth of the "audience" was small. I was having actual conversations with people on both platforms. On Facebook I connected with people from my past. I reengaged in relationships with people from high school and former jobs. This was, and to this day continues to be, gratifying.

Twitter was a different story. Twitter was like an ongoing debate. It was a running kibitzing session much like a tailgate party at a football game. Sometimes people debated news stories, other times it was about industry trends, but most often it was just lighthearted personal barbs exchanged among relative strangers in (at that time) 140 characters. For people who don't value relationships, this would be considered a waste of time.

Living in Miami and being a New York Jets fan is like wandering through a lion's den covered in a steak suit. In August 2007, I engaged in a running debate with several Dolphin's fans about who had a better football team. This pointless exercise served as my introduction to a Miami lawyer named Brian Tannebaum.

Tannebaum and I placed a friendly wager of a lunch on the Jets vs. Dolphins game played September 7, 2008. The Jets won, and a couple of weeks later, I met Tannebaum in person for the first time. In the decade-plus since that lunch, we have referred thousands of dollars in business to each other. We have spent time together socially. We've partaken in one another's life events. And we've become good friends. This is a relationship that never would have happened if not for social media.

Don't Start Fights on Social Media

As I write this, people are aggressively savaging each other on every platform. Fake accounts, known as *bots,* amplify political messages and, with pinpoint accuracy, those messages antagonize people into arguments with their "friends." The result: People hide behind a keyboard and verbally assault folks they grew up with because of an opinion about a political candidate.

You will never know about most of the business you lose because of social media stupidity. Here is a case study that provides a stellar example.

A client reached out to me and invited me to lunch. The topic: Investing in hotels. My client represented a businessman who invested in commercial real estate. This investor wanted to break into the hotel industry and he wanted a relationship with Marriott. The lunch was great, and my client and his client were cordial and professional. I agreed to reach out to my contacts in the hotel business and with Marriott and surface some opportunities.

About two weeks after that lunch I was scrolling through Facebook when I stumbled upon a particularly heated "discussion" about politics. I was shocked to discover the investor represented by my client verbally blasting people for their political opinion. He wasn't making a fact-based argument. He was launching into a personal attack, complete with profanity, on a public Facebook post.

This is not someone I want to be around. It is definitely not someone I want to introduce to my contacts at a conservative company like Marriott. Why? There are many reasons but the most important is his lack of judgement. If this man is willing to personally berate someone in an open forum, he will do it to my friends, clients, and other investors. I'm not willing to expose my contacts to that possibility.

I passed on the business opportunity and the exposure to a potentially volatile personality. I told my client the reason but I'm sure he didn't share my thoughts with the investor.

My purpose for addressing this phenomenon with you is strictly from a business development standpoint. I'm focused on helping you develop relationships. I want you to sell more of whatever it is you sell. That's why I can say, with peace and love, STOP PISSING PEOPLE OFF on social media!

Follow the advice of Vito Corleone in *The Godfather*: "Never tell anybody outside the family what you're thinking again." You don't sell products and services to people by arguing with them about politics, how to raise their kids, or religion. You wouldn't go up to someone in a sales meeting and say: "I heard you voted for that idiot governor. What were you thinking? You must be stupid. He's a criminal." Yet I see people do that everyday on social media.

Want to know what's worse? When you do it on Facebook, LinkedIn, or Twitter and a prospect does a search before meeting with you, sees it, and decides you're too irrational to work with.

I love freedom of speech. I love the Bill of Rights. But arguing with someone on a volatile subject on social media will hurt your income if you're in sales. There are no two ways about it.

How to Develop Relationships with Social Media

I'm going to share the value of a few social media platforms for the purposes of relationship development. That's what the 60 Second Sale system is all about (Figure 9.1). Make no mistake, you can completely destroy a relationship on social media in 60 seconds. Consider the guidance here to be your guide to relationship initiation and growth. However, much like a doctor, your underlying credo must be to, first, do no harm.

YouTube

We can all have our own television station. Setting up your own YouTube channel is fast and easy. If you've got a mobile telephone

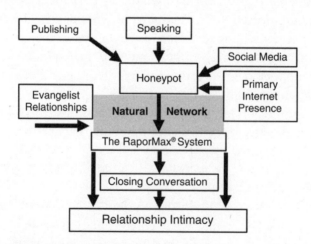

FIGURE 9.1   Social Media Creates Curiosity

with a camera, you can upload a video to YouTube in minutes after you finish shooting it. But treating video on YouTube like a television show would be a mistake. On YouTube, you should have conversations with the people in your audience.

Following the MAD (message, audience, delivery system) formula and the results of your Ideal Relationship Targeting 21 interview, you should highlight issues of concern to your ideal clients and have conversations with them on video. You should also have conversations about issues in your RaporMax® system calendar. Any topic appropriate for an article is also good for a video.

There is a distinct advantage to YouTube compared to other video platforms. YouTube is a fantastic search engine. Each day people search YouTube for things directly related to the value you provide. If you want to find a great starting point for relationship development with YouTube, make a list of the most frequently asked questions you receive. Answer those questions, one at a time, one video at a time.

If you need more material, look through articles you've written in the past and break them down into smaller pieces and record videos on each of those topics. One or two videos each week is a great way to keep your channel active.

If you find you are good at making videos and you enjoy it, you can create a video each day and leverage this platform as one of your key relationship initiation tools. Here is a step-by-step guide to using YouTube for relationship development in less than 20 minutes per day.

Step One: Create a content calendar.

Monday is FAQ day. That's the day you answer the most frequently asked questions you've received. Each Monday, answer a new question.

Tuesday is value presentation day. This is the day you present the value you provide for your clients. Each Tuesday you cover an additional way you provide value.

Wednesday is industry update day. Each Wednesday, you discuss something happening in your industry. Share your opinions.

Thursday is timesaving Thursday. Each Thursday you share a tip about how to do something that saves time. It doesn't matter if your product or service has nothing to do with time management or productivity. You are a successful business leader and people always want keys to success. Time management is one of the things that plagues most executives today. Help people save time. Those videos will always be in demand.

Friday is fun Friday. Each Friday, record a video of you having fun. This is a chance for you to demonstrate your humanity. People like to be in other people's business. Give them a chance to live vicariously through you.

That is an example of a content calendar I created for a client who owns an event planning company. This person shoots 20 videos each month, all in one day. The videos are about 2 to 3 minutes in length. It takes about 3 hours to get the month's videos shot. Editing is minimal and takes less than 5 minutes per video. That's 15 minutes total time invested per video.

Step Two: Write a detailed description of your video for YouTube. This description should be about 10 sentences and should be exactly what the video is about, why it's valuable, and what's in it for the viewer.

At the bottom of the description, always include a link to your Primary Internet Presence and an offer of your honeypot via a link to a dedicated page with opt-in information.

Step Three: Create a special video that offers your honeypot. In that video, "sell" the free information in the honeypot to the viewer. Why do they need this information? What's in it for them? What bad things will happen if they don't receive the information in the honeypot?

Using YouTube tools, embed a link to a honeypot offer into each video. This is different and in addition to putting the information in the YouTube description. YouTube offers the ability to add a link in the video to another video. The video you link to should be the video of you pitching your honeypot. In this stand-alone honeypot offer video, you give out website information so people can get the honeypot. This way you have two opportunities to capture information from YouTube viewers.

Step Four: Post the video everywhere you can. Embed it on your primary internet presence with a transcript. Send out links to it on other social media websites. Tweet about it along with a link to the video.

These are just a few of the ways you can leverage YouTube to initiate relationships. Remember your goal: Drive people to your honeypot so you can capture their contact information, enroll them in the RaporMax® System, and follow up.

Providing valuable information in video is a great way to start a relationship. I consider YouTube an essential resource for everyone interested in dominating their industry as a sales leader.

LinkedIn

LinkedIn is an intriguing opportunity for everyone. Here are five steps to leveraging it with a minimal investment of time:

1. *Fully develop your profile.* List as much detail as you possibly can about each role you have held and currently hold. Include any video, research papers, and a link to your honeypot right in your main bio.

2. *Research the leaders of your ideal client companies.* Try to connect with them on LinkedIn through connections you have in common. Follow those companies and their leaders so you are kept up to date on any news.

3. *Join groups that contain your ideal clients.* (These are defined by your Ideal Relationship Targeting 21 interview.) Participate as much as possible in discussions.

4. *Send automatic notifications.* Set up your profile to send out notifications each time you post an article on your primary internet presence in real time.

5. *Post entire articles you've written on LinkedIn.* Use at least a 30-day delay because you do not want to confuse search engines on the original source of the content. You can repurpose articles and video from your primary internet presence, your email newsletter, and published articles. Always include a link to where the article originally appeared, and always include a link to your honeypot.

LinkedIn is an extraordinary research tool. Explore it. Please do not use it to send messages to random people. Be judicious in using LinkedIn to communicate directly with people.

FACEBOOK

Facebook is a cesspool of egomaniacal, insular gasbags who enjoy being around people who think and act just like them. This makes it perfect for targeting people who will buy your products and services if you have a budget for advertising.

Don't use your personal page for business promotion. Use your personal page for photos of the kids or connecting with high school classmates with whom you've lost touch. If you want to add those people to your RaporMax® System, go ahead, but connect with those folks personally first – via Facebook Messenger and offline.

Set up a Facebook business page. Then post messages each day using the information gained from your Ideal Relationship Targeting 21 interviews. Keep in mind your message topics on Facebook will need to appeal more directly to the emotions of the reader than messages on your primary internet presence. This is because Facebook has a collection of people who invest time in the platform because they want their opinion validated. This is not a platform where people do research or seek objective information.

Join groups of people who have opinions similar to those folks with your ideal client profile. Frequently invite people from those groups to get your honeypot via a link to that web page. If you want to become fully invested in Facebook, you will want to create a separate and even more focused honeypot to offer to people from this platform.

The one area where Facebook has a significant advantage is in live video. This aspect of the platform is fantastic for creating video (with the same guidelines I've offered for YouTube) but doing it in real time from an event or speaking engagement. Promote this real-time event well in advance in the groups you've joined and make it a regular event. Think of it as having your own TV show. Make the show happen live at the same day and time each week and you will slowly build viewership. Once the live show is over, it will live on your Facebook page forever as a recorded video.

If you want to invest the time and effort to do Facebook Live video and target suspects with it, this platform makes sense. If you don't want to put in that work, or if you have limited time, Facebook is probably not for you.

The most powerful way to leverage Facebook is to invest in advertising on that platform. Use the information from your IRT 21 interview to target your ideal clients and then work with an expert to create ads they will see every time they log-in to Facebook. This is Facebook's business model and it works if you have an advertising budget and access to an expert in social media advertising.

TWITTER

I used to love Twitter. Today, not so much. There is a danger that Twitter might be the next MySpace. However, social media is so fickle that this platform could turn around and become hot again.

Here are the most productive ways to use Twitter:

Twitter is a great place to get breaking news – with a grain of salt. If you are in a fast-moving industry, follow the influencers on Twitter, create a list of them, and run through that feed a couple of times each day. Keep in mind, the information on Twitter comes so quickly it is often inaccurate.

Use Twitter to follow news media personalities and communicate with them. Almost everyone in the media – producers, editors, reporters – Tweet. Follow them and Tweet at them (use their Twitter "handle" in messages). You might be able to create an ongoing dialogue and develop a relationship.

Become a Twitter personality. Use Twitter to send links to the content from your primary internet presence. Once every 10 messages send a link to the web page that offers your honeypot. You can use a service to automate and schedule your Tweets. If you have time, this is a strategy that will drive some traffic to your primary internet presence. How much traffic? That depends on what happens with Twitter as a platform.

Keep an eye on Twitter. If it becomes hot again, jump in. Otherwise, only consider it if you have no other ways to invest your time.

INSTAGRAM

On Instagram you can share photos, photo "stories" (like a slideshow), and brief video.

The value of Instagram to your sales strategy is dependent on your industry. If you work in a visual field, this may be one of your primary tools for sales. I've worked with business leaders and sales professionals in the following industries to successfully leverage Instagram:

1. Artists: Share photos of your work. Nothing sells like a sample.
2. Food sales: We eat with our eyes. Feed us with photos.
3. Event and catering professionals: Photos of people having fun in an elegant setting are attractive to everyone. Who doesn't like fun?
4. Weight loss and fitness: Use Instagram for before-and-after photos, testimonials, and how-to videos.
5. Consultants, experts, and coaches: Give your best advice via Instagram video, succinctly.
6. Day care: Show kids learning, making friends, and enjoying themselves.
7. Education: Brief, aspirational videos of people graduating and being congratulated inspire action.
8. Landscaping: Before-and-after photos. "See how great your property can look!"
9. Car detailing: Another great before and after opportunity. Dirty mess becomes a renewed, refreshed, and revived sports car.
10. Restaurant: Selfie promotion. Show a selfie with a member of the staff and win a free dessert.

These are 10 examples of how I've used Instagram with my clients to attract interest. The key, of course is to offer the honeypot. You do this in Instagram by placing a link in your bio and reminding people, with each post, that they need to go to your Instagram bio and click on the link to get the "Free Report."

The challenge with Instagram is that the access to the honeypot offer is two steps removed from the media – you have to go from a great photo or a compelling succinct video to a different location – the bio – to get the honeypot offer. The converse is also true. If people work that hard to get the honeypot, they are going to be excellent prospects.

Please keep in mind anytime you use a photo or a video of another person, you should get their permission in advance.

If you are in a highly visual field, Instagram is a good vehicle to attract suspects and convert them.

What about Everything Else?

I left out several other social media platforms. I may have left out one (or many) of your favorites. The reason: time and proof of return on investment.

If you are an individual sales professional, a solo entrepreneur, or an independent professional, you may want to skip social media all together. If you have some time to invest, definitely leverage YouTube and LinkedIn.

If you have a social media team or the resources to hire free-lancers, follow the guidance on each of the forms of social media as outlined here. Once you've worked on those, you can look at other social platforms and experiment. The guidance I've included here is based on results I've seen from my business and my clients' businesses. As I've said a few times, when it comes to sales, I like sure things.

60 Second Actions

- Make a list of the most commonly asked questions you receive about the value you provide, your business, and your industry. Answer them in a video and post it on YouTube.
- Fully develop your profile on LinkedIn. Update your role and responsibilities as they evolve.
- Connect your website (primary internet presence) to LinkedIn. Turn on notifications for posts so everyone on LinkedIn knows when you post a new article.
- Using at least a 30-day delay, post entire articles you've written. You can repurpose content from your primary internet presence, your email newsletter, and published articles. Always include a link to where the article originally appeared, and always include a link to your honeypot.
- Use LinkedIn to follow your target companies. Research and connect with people from those companies on LinkedIn.

Chapter 10

ACTION Speaks Louder Than Words

60 Second Summary

If you want to take your sales to the next level, you can automate conversion from suspects to prospects with advertising. But you cannot use the most common form of advertising. You must use advertising that motivates people to take action – within the first 60 seconds.

Most ads are expensive. This chapter shares how and why the best ads really are free and why you as an individual sales executive need to think about advertising.

This chapter will force you to think differently about what you do. We turn you into the ultimate product and help people connect with you first.

What's in This Chapter for You?

You'll discover that advertising is the ultimate leverage because you pay to target your ideal client, offer them something they want and need – your honeypot – and then you can deepen the relationship until they become a client.

Most ads fail because they focus on building a brand. This chapter gives you the step-by-step guide to writing an action ad. That means you'll attract attention, captivate the audience, tempt them to make a decision, inform them what will happen if they don't act, offer them something, and nurture them so they feel good about what they've done.

The key concept you will discover in this chapter is that you are really the product. If you are a business leader, you have to get people to buy you before they agree to work for you or use your service or product. If you are a sales executive, they buy you before they buy what you're selling. If you are an independent professional, you might be the best lawyer or the best CPA or the best financial advisor nobody's heard of. You'll discover how to change that.

The Best Ad Is What They Say About You

I'm in Baltimore, Maryland, and I'm winding up a speech to a group of entrepreneurs. I'm on a roll but I can tell it's time to offer my honeypot. I have complete clarity of purpose, and the only reason I'm in front of this audience is to see who I can help and offer assistance to them.

Mid-sentence, I stop ...

"You know, I almost forgot, I have something for you. I have prepared a special report just for this group. The title is: 'Five Mistakes Smart Entrepreneurs Make in Sales ... And How to Avoid Them.' If you'd like a copy, pass your business cards to the center aisle and I will collect them. Pass them over now. But listen. This information is so valuable I only want to give it to people who are ready to make changes. So if you're ready to change the way you do things, pass your business card over."

The next day I get back to the office and I send the free report to each of the attendees. I also send 35 separate testimonial letters from entrepreneurs. The testimonials are better than any advertising copy I could write. They talk about my character and they talk about the return on investment from working with me.

A few days later, I call everyone who received this information. The five people who sign up to work with me all cite the testimonials as the most important factor in their decision. They said it was what convinced them to trust me and they each express how ready they are for change in their sales approach.

This is a typical result from a speaking engagement to an audience of about 200 people. There is yet another way to receive these results. That method is to advertise to the exact target audience and give them a chance to opt in for the honeypot.

As an individual sales executive, entrepreneur, or business leader, you need to think about advertising because it is now an option at all budget levels and it allows you to convert suspects to prospects with leverage. That is the focus of our discussion in this chapter.

Branding Is Expensive

When you watch television, you see lots of dumb money ads. While in most cases this spending should not be taken as an indictment of the people who pay for the advertising, the money could be invested in more productive ways.

Most television advertising is designed to generate *brand awareness*. This means they run ads to make you think and feel favorably about a name – like Coke or Cadillac. While this will work with enough repetition, it is very expensive to run the advertisement often enough with enough reach to have an impact on purchase behavior.

With the 60 Second Sale system, you don't need to run ads with wide and repeat exposure because you know exactly who to reach and you motivate them to take action and convert from suspect to prospect.

Brand advertising attempts to motivate the audience member to convert from suspect directly to client without creating a relationship and building trust. The frequency of exposure is the advertiser's attempt over time to build a relationship – but that relationship is with a brand and not with a person.

I have my clients focus on a different formula for advertising.

ACTION™ Advertising

ACTION is an acronym. It stands for:

Attract attention.
Captivate the audience.
Tempt the audience to make a decision.
Inform the audience what will happen if they don't act now.
Offer them something.
Nurture them after they've taken action.

Let's break down each of the elements of ACTION™ advertising.

ATTRACT ATTENTION

This is the 60 Second Sale in a microcosm. You have to connect with the ideal client in 60 seconds or less to attract their attention. To do so, you must think in headlines. What can you say to capture your ideal client's attention?

There are five headline formulas that are most effective for capturing attention. Each formula connects with the audience member on an emotional level.

Formula One: "How to ..." This headline works because it feeds on the desire we all have to achieve a goal.

- How to make money in today's stock market
- How to lose 15 pounds in time for summer beach season
- How to get a college degree in less than three years

Formula Two: "Secrets revealed." This headline works because it plays on our natural curiosity.

- Super model reveals secrets to a perfect body in just 15 minutes per day
- Investment secrets your financial advisor doesn't want you to know
- Scientist discovers secret formula that reverses skin aging

Formula Three: "Mistakes." This headline focuses on the need for the audience member to avoid fear and pain.

- Five mistakes most business owners make with their taxes that get them into hot water with the IRS
- Three mistakes most parents make that kill their child's self-esteem
- Seven most common mistakes smart golfers make ... and how to avoid them

Formula Four: "Who else ..." This headline highlights the need each of us has to be included in a group or an activity. This need for inclusion is basic human nature.

- Who else wants to save $50 per week on groceries?
- Who else wants to discover the simple script for instantly attracting that special someone?
- Who else wants to eliminate embarrassing foot odor with an all-natural treatment?

Formula Five: "They all laughed." This headline formula helps the audience member avoid embarrassment and shame.

- They all laughed when I got so fat, but you should see their faces now that I'm a size two.
- Everyone laughed the first time I took the stage ... until I started to dance.
- My friends laughed when I told them I was day-trading ... until I pulled up in a Ferrari.

These headline formulas work because they focus on the emotions of greatest concern to your ideal client.

Captivate the Audience

My favorite type of ad is called an *advertorial*. This is an article you pay to place in a magazine or an event program or even in a newspaper. Most times the article will have the words ADVERTISEMENT plastered over the top, but it is still effective.

In an advertorial, you tell a story to captivate the reader. The story should be one where something happens to the main character and your free report (honeypot) saves the day. The more compelling the story, the greater the chance you'll draw in the reader.

When you develop the story, it should be with your ideal client in mind.

For example: If you are selling locksmith services to commercial buyers in a hotel industry trade magazine, don't use a story of a mom and her kids being locked out of the car in a bad part of town. Instead, use the story of a chief security officer of a hotel company needing to find out who was in a room when some jewels were stolen. He can't interrogate the lock because he doesn't have your product – which makes every entrance downloadable via encrypted internet access.

Stories work great to captivate during longer-form advertisements like advertorials, or television and radio commercials. But pay-per-click or social media advertisements are outstanding for our purposes. For these highly targeted ads, you simply double down on the headline and mix and match (because you don't have a lot of characters to work with). Examples (underlined part is the top line):

- ◆ Free Report Reveals: How to make money in today's stock market.
- ◆ Millionaire Shares: Investment secrets your financial advisor doesn't want you to know.
- ◆ Your Golf Pro Hates Me: I want to give you the seven most common mistakes smart golfers make...and how to avoid them.

No matter how much or how little space you have to work with, you need to pull people in quickly and captivate them.

Tempt the Audience to Make a Decision

You'll notice in the short-form ads above I put the text about the free report early in the copy. The reason I did that was to temp the reader to make a decision. I want them to read the ad and think, "Hey, free report. I want that."

In a longer ad, the free report is the solution to the problem the main character is facing. After you tell the story, you insert text that says:

"This will never happen to you once you read our free report titled...."

You're not offering the report at this point but just teasing the fact that reading it will solve or prevent the problem.

Inform the Audience What Will Happen If They Don't Act Now

Introducing the consequences of inaction is important to getting the audience to act with urgency.

This is as simple as adding a line in the ad that says: "Don't wait to get your hands on this report because if you do you might lose...."

The more succinct you can make this, the better. Make it brief but powerful.

Offer Them Something

This is where you tell them how to get the honeypot right now. Don't be shy. Tell them how to get it (see Figure 10.1).

Nurture Them after They've Taken Action

This step is not part of the advertisement but part of the follow-up.

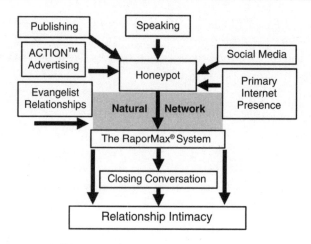

Figure 10.1　ACTION™ Makes Advertising Work

Make sure the email that contains the honeypot congratulates them on taking the right action. It should praise them for doing the smart thing. They need to feel great about getting information that will help them save the day.

Types of Ads

I've mentioned *advertorials* – long-form article-style ads you can pay to run. These are my favorite because they can educate and entertain in the same way as an article but be much harder hitting on the call to action – the offer of the honeypot.

I have also mentioned pay-per-click and social media pay-per-action ads. The entire ad will only be three lines long. It is essentially a doubled-up headline and a link to a web page where people can opt in to get your honeypot. It is very short but every word matters.

Video ads are also powerful. Follow the ACTION formula but use it in narrative form as you tell the story on a video. You could do a television style production where actors play out the story, but that gets expensive.

How to Pay for Ads

If you are an individual sales executive working for a company, you're saying to yourself: "This would be really valuable at positioning me as an expert, but I can't possibly pay for ads. My company will never go for that. They'd rather just have me cold call."

There are a few ways you can use this ACTION™ advertising strategy and make it work for you:

- ◆ Shoot a video ad that you narrate and have it ready to go. Use it on the homepage of your primary internet presence.
- ◆ When you offer to give people an article, any article for publishing, offer them the video ad as a "bonus." People won't see it as an ad but as an offer of valuable material.
- ◆ Offer to help out as a volunteer for an event in exchange for running an advertorial in their program or your video on their website.
- ◆ Help recruit people into a trade organization in exchange for advertising.
- ◆ If possible, exchange your product or service for advertising when possible and ethical.

Natural ACTION™ Ads – Testimonials

Testimonials are one form of powerful advertising available to you right now, for free. A testimonial is an endorsement of your work by someone who has no financial interest in your success. You may not think of it as advertising, but when someone gives you a true, heartfelt testimonial, no copywriter can provide anything more valuable.

Testimonials attract attention, captivate the audience, tempt them to take action, inform the audience what will happen if they don't act, offer you as an option, and, by their very nature, are a nurturing way to help people through a rough time.

How Testimonials Attract Attention

If you are doing a great job with the 60 Second Sale system, you are developing deep relationships quickly and in large numbers. These are people who recognize the value you provide – both personally and professionally. You are going to ask each of them for a testimonial.

Most people don't do this. The reasons vary from being shy, to just forgetting to ask, to not wanting to do the work to help a client put together a good testimonial. That's good news for you because when people see testimonials on your sales proposals, on your contracts, on your website, on your business cards, and on any advertising you do, they will stand out.

Since testimonials are rare, they stand out like a flashing sign that says: READ ME. That's why testimonials attract attention.

Testimonials captivate the audience because they showcase ordinary people – people just like your ideal client – doing remarkable things as a result of your work with them. Think about it: Somebody just like them, achieving results they want but never thought possible. That gives them hope and it draws them in.

A good testimonial will also tempt the audience to decide to take action by highlighting the emotions people felt before the transformation.

"I was intimidated by the sales process before I called Dave Lorenzo. I didn't know how to start a conversation. I didn't know how to get someone to say yes, and I really didn't want to ever make a cold call. Dave showed me a better way."

By their nature, testimonials highlight the consequences of inaction. They show transformation from a low point to success. The audience automatically sees themselves at a natural starting point – they may not consider it a low, but they definitely have a desire to improve. When they view the average person achieving above average growth, it triggers FOMO – fear of missing out – which is a powerful motivator.

While a testimonial doesn't make a direct call to action to the audience, it offers hope. I've worked with many people in the nutrition and physical fitness industry who engage a dietary coach or a personal trainer, and the minute they make the investment they immediately feel better about themselves. This is because they now have hope they never experienced before. This hope comes from seeing the results others have achieved and believing, "If they can do it, I can do it."

That's also the nurturing aspect of a testimonial. You cannot get your best clients to meet every new client, give them a hug, and say, "It's going to be okay." But that's what a testimonial does. It makes people feel like they are going to achieve their goal if they work with you. It is reassuring.

Types of Testimonials

In the 60 Second Sale system, we use five different types of testimonials.

Thwart Objections This testimonial directly addresses the objections people have to using your services. The best way to ask someone to provide you with this type of testimonial is to say to them:

> "Tell me about your biggest concern before we started working together. How do you feel about that now?"

Then record or write down exactly what they say.

Character Reference Anyone who has known you for a long time can give this type of testimonial. The references need to include the length of time that individuals have known you, an example of something they've seen you do that demonstrates good moral character, and then a blatant endorsement. Here's an example:

> "Catherine has worked with the community kitchen for 15 years. Each Thanksgiving she volunteers to feed homeless families at our shelter rather than spend the afternoon with her own family. Her dedication and commitment to the less fortunate in our community is unparalleled."

Industry or Community Credibility This is similar to the character reference but it is focused on credibility in your primary area of business focus. You are seeking testimonials from your peers. You need a good mix of people with high stature and people who are considered rank and file. The idea is to highlight your expertise. Here is an example:

> "As the president of the Tamiami Society of Accounting Professionals, I meet lots of CPAs. There is no one I'd trust more than Harold Smith. Harold is knowledgeable, dedicated, and ethical. He does the taxes for me and my business. He has my highest recommendation."

Urgency   When you tell people to take action, they hear you but they don't necessarily take it to heart. Having some testimonials that motivate people is incredibly valuable. Here's what an urgency inducing testimonial looks like:

> "I waited too long before calling Steve Klitzner for help. The IRS seized my tax refund, levied my bank account, and put a lien on my house. I could have avoided this if I had called Steve when I received the first letter. Through some great negotiating, everything was eventually straightened out. But if I had to do it all over again, I would have gotten Steve involved right from the beginning. Don't wait. Call him now."

These testimonials are essential because they provide third-party verification of the need to take action immediately.

Turnaround   This is a controversial type of testimonial. Many people will instruct you to never use it. That's the reason I love it so much. Think about the client with whom you'd gotten off to a rough start but now have an outstanding relationship. Have them talk about that.

This is important for three reasons:

1. It shows you are human and things sometimes get messed up. That builds credibility.
2. It encourages people to stick with you when times get tough.
3. You address tough subjects, in advance, vicariously.

Here is an example of a turnaround testimonial from my business:

> "Dave is a proponent of 'tough love' in his sales coaching. We got off to a rough start because he called me lazy and told me I was afraid to try new things. He was right, but it hurt hearing that. You may not like what Dave says or how he says it, but he is a genius when it comes to growing your business. My sales are up 175% this year and it is entirely a result of the work we are doing together."

Note the specifics in the improvement mentioned in this testimonial. That is key. Things were rough, but I achieved the goal. That is a trade-off most people will take – especially when things were rough because that was what drove the change.

Testimonial Signature

Testimonials are useless if they don't contain a signature. If you have a client write you a testimonial letter, it must be on their letterhead and signed by them. If you are going to use their testimonial in other places, the following items are a must:

◆ Full Name – first and last
◆ Position and company name
◆ City and state

Without this information, people will not believe your testimonial. Don't even bother using it. I shouldn't have to state this, but I will: Never fake a testimonial. Get written permission to use your client's words in all of your sales activities.

Here is some additional information you should include whenever possible:

◆ Photo of you with the person who gave the testimonial. Again, this adds credibility.
◆ Headshot of the person who gave the testimonial. If it is not possible for you to take a photo with the person, use their headshot.
◆ Video of the person saying the words they've written. This is the ultimate in credibility. If the person says it on camera, it is believable.

The Secret to Getting Great Testimonials

There is a secret to getting outstanding testimonials. Since you've read this far in this book, you can probably guess that I have a system for this process. Here it is.

Step One: Set the Table

When you begin work with clients, let them know that as a part of your relationship you will need feedback from them on the status of your relationship. This feedback will come in many forms. Each time you interact, you'll ask for informal feedback, but twice during your initial relationship, you will want formal feedback.

The first time you'll want formal feedback is when you deliver value. This might be when they purchase a product and have used it successfully for 90 days or when you've delivered a service and they are happy with the results. At that time, you will have someone – preferably a member of your team and not you personally – interview them.

The second time you'll get feedback is when they finish their work with you. At that point, you will send them a survey and you'll ask them to fill it out.

You tell them this upfront because you want them to be prepared to participate in this process.

STEP TWO: THE INTERVIEW

After you've delivered value to the client, you arrange for her to be interviewed by a member of your team. Always ask permission to make an audio recording of the interview and save that recording. If you can video this interview, it will be even more valuable. Here are the questions you must ask:

- ◆ Please give us your full name and the spelling of it.
- ◆ We are going to interview you to get your feedback on the work we did together. Do we have your permission to use this information to improve our service?
- ◆ May we also share your thoughts with future clients in our sales process?
- ◆ Please describe the work we did together (or describe the product you purchased).
- ◆ Why did you decide to work with us (buy this product)?
- ◆ How did you feel before you worked with us? How do you feel now?
- ◆ What problem did we (or our product) solve? Why was solving this problem so important?
- ◆ If you had it to do all over again, would you work with us (buy this product)?
- ◆ Why?
- ◆ Would you recommend this product to a friend?
- ◆ Why?

- Look into the camera as if it was your friend and tell them why they should work with us (if not on camera, look at me).
- May we transcribe this interview and send excerpts to you so you can confirm them and place them on your letterhead with your signature?

This entire interview process takes about 15 minutes. Although I prefer video, this can be done over the telephone.

STEP THREE: CONFIRMATION

Transcribe the interview and clean up the transcript to make it read well in writing. Format it as a letter with a signature line for the client. Send it to the client and ask him to place it on his letterhead and sign it.

STEP FOUR: SURVEY

At the conclusion of your work with the client (or after the purchase of your product), send the client a survey with a postage-paid return envelope. You are going to ask similar questions to the interview. Here is a sample, along with a cover letter explaining the process.

CLIENT NAME
CLIENT ADDRESS

DATE
Re:

Dear PREFIX CLIENT-LAST-NAME:

Thank you for allowing me the honor of working with you.

I hope you were happy with my efforts on your behalf. In my continuing effort to improve, I would like your candid feedback. Enclosed is an evaluation form with a self-addressed stamped envelope. Please take a moment to fill out the evaluation and drop it in the mail. Your observations are greatly appreciated.

I take great pride in the fact that many of my clients are word-of-mouth referrals from family, friends, trusted colleagues, and former clients. With this in mind, I hope that you will contact me if you need assistance in the future.

Our immediate work together is over; however, I would like to think of you as my client for life.

I encourage you to call me with *any business question or matter*, even if it deals with an issue outside of the things we've worked on together. I may still be able to give helpful advice, and I can always find another expert to help you in areas that are outside of my area of focus.

Call me when you don't know who to call.

Once again, thank you for the trust you've placed in me.

Sincerely,
Your Name Here

Client Evaluation

Please Circle Your Selection

How would you rate the service you received?	Bad	Moderate	Good
How would you rate the solution to your original problem?	Bad	Moderate	Good
How well did I keep you informed of the status of our work together?	Bad	Moderate	Good
How effectively did I explain the process involved in our work together?	Bad	Moderate	Good
How would you assess my knowledge of your business?	Bad	Moderate	Good
How would you rate my overall performance?	Bad	Moderate	Good

Please describe the best aspects of my service during our work together.

What else would you like to share with me about our relationship or about the work we did together?

Will you allow me to share this evaluation with other potential clients?	Yes	No
Would you recommend me to a friend or colleague?	Yes	No

There are a few important aspects to this survey:

- *The choices are not particularly sophisticated.* The reason for this is because you want the client to be prompted to write about anything they experienced that was extremely positive. By making the choices for answers in the survey mundane, we encourage the client to elaborate about extremely valuable service.

- *We prompt the client for referrals in both the cover letter and in the survey letter.* We discuss this in detail in the networking chapter, but it is important to note that a client who refuses to give you a testimonial will never refer you to someone else. Think about that for a moment. If your client won't take a few minutes and talk about you in a positive way, or write about a positive experience with you, he is never going to go out of his way to promote you to a friend or colleague.

- *This is personal.* You are not asking about the service received from the company. You are asking about service the client received from you. Remember, we are building relationships. That's you and them. To them you are the company.

You Are the Real Product

We have discussed a couple of ideas for advertising and leveraging advertising to convert suspects to prospects. We discussed testimonials and how to collect them. You are going to use the testimonials to help convert suspects into prospects and prospects into clients (Figure 10.1). You may be wondering why advertising is important to you, because you are an individual trying to close more deals.

Think of it this way: You are a one-person army. You can go into battle with a knife, with a pistol, with a shotgun, with a machine gun, or in a fully armored vehicle with an automatic assault weapon that fires 6,000 rounds per minute. Networking is the knife. Writing is the shotgun. Speaking is the machine gun. Advertising is the fully armed and armored vehicle. You select the right tool for the job, but you need to have all of them in your arsenal.

60 Second Actions

- ◆ Practice writing advertisements and show them to your best clients. Make notes about what resonates.
- ◆ Seek advertorial placement in publications where you can barter.
- ◆ Test headlines with ads on social media and pay-per-click search engine ads. Work with experts on placement, but don't invest large dollars until you are certain you will receive a positive return on investment.
- ◆ Set up a testimonial system, beginning with an interview process.
- ◆ Do one interview each week.
- ◆ Begin sending out surveys with the cover letter.

Chapter 11

How to Be Great at Networking Even If You Hate People

60 Second Summary

Networking by joining groups and associations makes sense for many sales executives, independent professionals, and entrepreneurs. You need to approach networking with a plan, and you need a step-by-step guide to make it work.

In this chapter you will discover which organizations you should join and which you should walk away from.

You will also uncover the steps necessary to make any networking meeting instantly productive.

Doing your homework ahead of time will help you make the most out of your next business networker. This chapter contains a comprehensive guide to targeting the right people and getting an introduction to them.

What's in This Chapter for You?

This chapter will help you select the ideal networking groups. Every group is productive, but not every group will be productive for you. In fact, you may not want to invest your time with networking at all.

By the time you've finished reading this chapter, you'll be able to determine which networking group you want to join and how to make the most out of it. You will also have a foolproof follow-up system you can use to add people to your network after each meeting.

These people will be predisposed to receiving your honeypot and any additional information you want to send them.

The key concept you will discover in this chapter is the five-step process that leads to business after an introduction at a networking event.

Speed Networking: A Fast Trip to Nowhere

The definition of strategic audacity: Move to a city where you don't know anyone, start a business, and have a baby in the same 90-day time frame. Writing that sentence today, I realize how brave I was. When I lived it back then, it was stupidity.

But I survived because I was motivated and I ran, as fast as I could, to as many networking meetings as I could. When you don't know anyone, and security won't let you into the office of the CEO of any company in town, you have to find people to talk to in order to be able to sell things.

One day an email came into my inbox that promoted something called *speed networking*. Somebody got the idea that speed dating was not awkward and embarrassing enough, so we needed that fast-paced humiliation extended to business. Since I needed to meet people, I thought this would be a great opportunity to meet lots of people quickly.

I arrived in the meeting room at the venue a little early. There were 20 chairs lined up like a game of musical chairs was about to start. On the back of each chair was the letter A. Opposite those chairs were an additional 20 chairs with a letter B on the back of each. On each side of the aisle between the chairs was a poster board that read:

Rules for Speed Networking
- Each team will have two minutes to network.
- A horn will blow signaling the beginning of the two minutes.
- During minute one row A will speak.
- A bell will ring, signaling the end of the first minute.
- During minute two, row B will speak.
- When the horn blows, row A slides down while row B remains in place.
- Speed networking ends when you have visited with everyone twice.

I sat in a chair marked row A. As all the chairs filled up, I noticed that everyone was silent. I asked the person next to me why nobody was talking. "They don't want to use up any of their good lines," was the response.

Once all the chairs were full, a woman stood next to me and pushed the button on the loudest air horn I've ever heard. The aerosol chemical from the canister squirted out and burned my neck and the sound immediately rendered me deaf. I was so startled by the noise, I jumped out of the seat, stumbled over the easel with the poster board, and fell to the floor.

I scrambled back to a seat because I had already wasted 15 seconds. Since I could not hear what was being said, I simply smiled, nodded, and shook hands with everyone while exchanging business cards. My partners at each station, for both rounds, gladly talked for the entire two minutes. Nobody found my lack of conversation odd. In fact, they seemed to prefer it.

During the days that followed, I received at least 10 telephone calls from people with whom I interacted during speed networking. Each of them seemed to think I was interested in buying something from them. There was the artist who offered a commissioned portrait of me for my office conference room (I worked from home). Next, I received calls from a landscaper and a pool maintenance company (I lived in a high-rise condo). I also was called by a cosmetic sales representative and a chiropractor (my back was fine and my face looks better *au naturel*).

That entire speed networking exercise was destined to fail because there was no time to see if there was a possibility for a connection. All the chamber of commerce did was set the attendees up for a series of cold calls. All I received from this event was freezer burn on my neck, mild hearing loss, and a series of sales pitches.

This story is indicative of the approach most people take to networking. Everyone is in "send mode." Nobody is looking to provide value to anyone else. If you have enough of these experiences, you'll begin to hate networking events – but even worse, you'll hate people.

You know, from our discussion of external orientation, that's not the way to initiate a relationship.

Not wanting to waste the time spent at speed networking, and since my hearing had returned, I rewarded the people who called me with some business opportunities. No, I didn't buy anything from them myself. But I did find out who their ideal client would be.

I introduced the artist to the man who lived across the hall from me. He was the business manager for a large family trust. He thought it would be great to have a portrait done of the family patriarch.

The landscaper and pool maintenance company owner each came to my condo building and I introduced them to the chief engineer. They both submitted proposals for their services.

My wife hosted a party for the cosmetic sales lady and received a basket full of makeup for doing so, and the chiropractor was looking for a doubles partner. My wife's uncle was an excellent tennis player, so I made that introduction.

In the process of making these connections, the folks who originally wanted to sell to me wound up looking to help me. Over time, these folks referred me to businesses with sales teams and I was able to develop some valuable relationships as a result.

Having an external orientation is the most important aspect of the 60 Second Sale system, and that comes through loud and clear in networking. Even if you attend an awful meeting, as long as you connect with one person, you have an opportunity to make that relationship productive for both parties. The key is in the follow-up.

Here is your step-by-step guide to networking strategy and follow-up.

The Ultimate Guide to Networking

You need to know who will be in the meeting before you attend. That's not as difficult as it sounds. The easiest way to find out who will be at the meeting is to call the organizer and ask who has registered to attend. Explain why you want to know. Here is a script you can use:

> "Hello this is Dave Lorenzo (use your name, not mine). I'm attending the monthly lunch on Thursday, and there are a few people I like to connect with. Can you help me find out if they have registered to attend the lunch?"

When the event organizer on the other end of the phone offers to help, ask about someone specific.

> "I'm looking to meet Robert Reynolds, President of Tamiami Bank and Trust, because I have several clients who need lines of credit for their professional practices. I think I can send him these referrals."

I did three important things in that exchange. I used a specific name, a title, and a company, and I explained why I want to make the connection. I do this because:

1. I might get lucky and get the person on the phone to introduce me directly to the target, even if he isn't attending the meeting.
2. I mention the title and company because the event organizer might not know the president of the company but might know someone else who can be valuable.
3. I say why I want to meet the person because the organizer might not know anyone in that company but might know someone in a different firm who is just as valuable and can help with my objective.

You don't even need to wait for an event to use this strategy. If you belong to a business group – like a chamber of commerce – call up the membership director and use this approach. Make sure you do your research ahead of time. But it is the membership director's job to help you make connections. That's the way she delivers value to the members.

STARTING THE CONVERSATION

When you meet the target, you use the script for starting a conversation I introduced in Chapter 2. As a refresher, I've included it below.

Opening Question
◆ What do you do for a living? How did you get into that?

Question 1: How's Life?
◆ How is business (life)?
◆ What goals do you have for the next (month, year)? Or
◆ What are you working on right now? Or
◆ What are you most concerned about?

Question 2: What's It Mean to You?
◆ How will achieving that help you personally? Or
◆ Why is that so important to you? Or
◆ What will that mean for your life?

Question 3: What's Stopping You?
- ◆ What is keeping you from achieving your goals? Or
- ◆ What is keeping that from happening? Or
- ◆ What's holding you back?

Question 4: How Can I Help?
- ◆ Would you like some help with that? Or
- ◆ Who can I connect you with to help you?

Begin a conversation about who can help achieve this goal.

FIVE STEPS TO EFFECTIVE FOLLOW-UP
After you meet your intended target, you need to follow up in order to initiate the relationship. There are five steps to effective follow-up after meeting someone.

Step One: Send a Personal Email   Immediately after meeting the person, return to your computer and send the following email.

Subject line: Great Meeting You

Dear <name>,

It was a pleasure meeting you today at <name of event>. I enjoyed learning about <subject you discussed>.

There are several people I believe will be valuable connections for you. I'm going to reach out to them and see if we can get together for a proper introduction.

Below is my contact information for your files. <Attach your contact info or type it into the email>

I look forward to seeing you again soon.

Warm regards,
<Your Name>

Step Two: Send a Handwritten Note   The minute you hit send on your email, pull out a note card from your desk and jot a handwritten note to the person with whom you had a conversation. In that note, reference something you discussed and close with a pleasantry. The note doesn't have to be long. The note card doesn't have to be fancy – in fact, it can be a plain note card from a pack you purchase at a local convenience store or pharmacy.

After you write out the notecard, write the person's address on the envelope and hand write your return address. Then put an actual stamp on it – don't run it though the office postage meter.

The reason you do all these things by hand, yourself, is to show you are PERSONALLY interested in a relationship. This takes less than five minutes and it makes a great impression.

Note: This must be done immediately after meeting the person. It loses impact if you wait.

Step Three: Call to Ask a Question Few things are more flattering than demonstrating respect for someone's expertise. That's why, about one week later, you call contacts you've met and ask them a question related to what they do or the knowledge they have.

This should be an intelligent question, and the answer should be useful to you in some way. It can be a question about what someone does, it can be a question about an organization that a contact leads. It can be a question about someone or something you have in common.

The bottom line: You need to ask a question that makes the person feel: smart or connected or important or influential.

Step Four: Introduce the Contact to Someone Else About 10 days after meeting this person, schedule a meeting to introduce him to someone who is a prospective client or potential evangelist. Based on your initial conversation, you should be able to identify the ideal target for this opportunity. Once identified, reach out to the target, propose the meeting, then reach out to the person you met at the networking event and set it up.

Step Five: Send Your Honeypot and Add the New Contact to Your RaporMax® System After you have followed all of the steps above, make sure you enroll this prospect in your system exactly like everyone else you meet.

You want this person to receive all of your communication moving forward because you believe he will be a great client or an evangelist someday. Customize an email explaining how your system works and send the prospect your honeypot (see Figure 11.1).

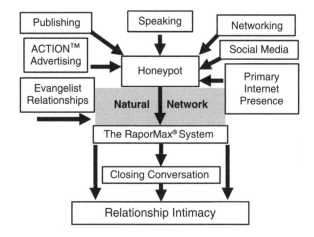

FIGURE 11.1   Networking Leads to Great Relationships

Give the Way You Want to Receive

Whenever I deliver a speech about networking to an audience, someone always raises a hand and says they get lots of referrals but none of them ever turn into clients. They lament the value of networking and they deride the practice of it as a tool. They express contempt, even hatred for people who attend networking events.

Their experiences are undoubtedly accurate, but their logic is flawed. The reason they don't receive quality referrals is because they don't pass quality referrals. That may be hard for some people to accept, but it is accurate.

You receive referrals in the same way you pass them.

Take the case of Hal, an attorney with a 150-attorney regional law firm. Hal stood up at a training session I was leading and made this exact statement:

> "People tell me they give out my name all the time. In fact, someone called me yesterday and told me he gave my name to the general counsel of a large company for a significant litigation matter. That guy will never call me. I don't know why, but these *referrals* never call."

I asked Hal how he referred people. He looked puzzled. I said: "When you want to send a client to a colleague, how do you connect the two of them?"

"Oh. I put three names in an email and send over that list with all the relevant contact information," Hal said.

"Why do you do it that way?" I asked.

"Because if things go badly, I don't want it to be a reflection upon me," was Hal's response.

In that moment, everyone in the room got it. Hal was the recipient of referrals in exactly the same way he was passing referrals. People were putting his name on a list with two other people, and when prospects receive that list, they know nothing more than they knew before they asked for the referral.

If you are going to send a list of names to someone who wants help, you should just send them an old-fashioned telephone book. You're doing them a disservice and you are doing yourself a disservice.

People refer you the way you teach them to refer you. When you pass a referral, you provide them with an example of how you want to receive referrals.

Providing names on a list is bad. Just as bad is mentioning a name in passing and then calling and telling the person you supposedly trust that you mentioned their name. You know how this goes:

"Hi, Dave. I was just having lunch with the CEO of Macro Software. She asked if I knew someone to help with salesforce effectiveness training. I mentioned your name."

That's not a referral. That is an invitation to make a cold call. I hate that. I'd rather not hear about this "mention." Why? Because when you call to follow-up, there is zero chance the prospective client will remember your name. If she did, she would have called you.

Those are two examples of wrong ways to pass referrals. There are three good ways to refer people. There are three ways to teach people to refer you. I've ranked them here:

- ◆ Good: Email introduction
- ◆ Better: Telephone connection
- ◆ Best: Personal meeting

EMAIL INTRODUCTION

If you are separated across the miles and you want to connect two people you think might be able to do business together, an email introduction is one option. Here's what that looks like:

Subject: Introduction for Confidential Investigations

Good afternoon, Al and Helen,

I'd like you to meet Marc Hurwitz. Marc owns a private investigation company named Crossroads Investigations. He is the person we discussed when I was in your office. You mentioned you wanted a referral to someone who you can trust with sensitive investigative work. Marc is a former CIA officer and he worked at the White House. He is a good friend of mine and I trust him with everything, especially sensitive information.

I encourage you both to visit Marc's website: https://xinvestigations.com

When you are ready to hire your next employee, I strongly encourage you to have Marc run a comprehensive background check on the candidate before you extend an offer. I personally do not engage anyone (whether it is a nanny for my kids or a service person for my home) without Marc checking them out.

In addition, Marc has interesting experience working in dangerous jurisdictions. If you happen to have clients who travel to areas of the world where kidnapping is a problem, those folks would be great people to introduce to him.

I'd like to set up a call to introduce you to Marc. Please let me know what days work for you.

Marc,

Al owns a law firm that focuses on estate planning for high-net worth people as well tax planning for family offices. His clients are sophisticated entrepreneurs.

Helen is the chief of staff at the firm and she manages the day-to-day operations.

Please let me know how I can help you connect.

Warm regards,
Dave Lorenzo

You'll notice I gave a detailed introduction of both parties. I explained the value of the relationship to both parties, and I offered to make a telephone connection of the parties. The reason I did it in this way is because I wanted to convey the level of trust I have in Marc to Al. I also didn't just fire off the email and think that was the end of it. I wanted to take things a step further and connect them via telephone because they are in different cities. Had we all been in the same city, I would have set up an in-person meeting for us.

Telephone Connection

A telephone connection is a better way to pass a referral for someone who is in a different city than the prospective client. You will need to set up an appointment in advance and then schedule the telephone call. On the call, you serve as a facilitator and make your "live" introduction in the same way you've made your email introduction. Then you let the two parties discuss how they can work together.

The telephone connection is better than a stand-alone email because of the personal touch, your voice connecting them. It conveys an even deeper level of trust.

Personal Meeting

The personal meeting is the best way to pass a referral. When you take the time to bring someone to my office, or bring someone to a breakfast or lunch we will have together, it shows me you really trust that person. You've taken time and made the effort to get everyone together. That demonstrates your commitment to the parties involved.

If you care about the people involved, if you want them to go the extra mile when they refer you, then you will go the extra mile and set up a personal meeting for the high-value relationships you have in business.

People will refer you the way you refer them. Always keep that in mind when you connect people.

You'll notice networking, and follow-up associated with it, requires a more personal approach than many of the other client attraction systems we have discussed. This is the reason why you have to be judicious in your selection of networking targets and in your selection of networking events.

How to Select the Best Groups for Business Networking

If you are new to a community or if you have a limited budget, business networking groups may be good way for you to connect with prospective clients and evangelists. There are dozens (if not hundreds) of groups you can join to meet new people and use the system already outlined. However, everyone has a capacity when it comes to new relationship connections within a narrow time frame.

My rule for business networking is simple. THREE. That's the number of new contacts you should hold yourself accountable for making at any single group meeting, and it is also the number of groups of which you should be a member at any given time.

This doesn't mean you should join three groups. It only means you should be a member of a maximum of three groups at one time. If you have the other client attraction systems working effectively, you may not need to become a member of any business groups at all.

If you decide you'd like to explore group memberships as a way to broaden your networking horizons, there are six types of groups available to you:

1. Client trade associations
2. General business groups
3. Civic groups
4. Charitable organizations
5. Educational groups
6. Structured networking groups

Each of these organizations provides a unique value proposition and may be worthwhile, depending on your goals and the amount of time and energy you have to invest in them.

Client Trade Associations

These are the best groups to join. They are full of people who are just like your ideal clients. If your ideal clients are CPAs, you should join the American Institute of Certified Public Accountants and a local chapter of that organization. If your best clients are financial advisors, you should join the National Association of Insurance and Financial Advisors and its local chapter.

Every meeting you attend with a trade association comprised of your best clients is a tremendous opportunity.

GENERAL BUSINESS GROUPS

This type of group is typically a local or regional chamber of commerce. These groups are good if you want to do the heavy lifting. By that I mean you have to filter through all the people in the organization who are NOT your ideal client in order to get to those who are your ideal client.

An advantage of this type of group is you will often have access to people in large companies. Big companies love to sponsor local chambers of commerce, and you will be able to access some decision makers as a result.

CIVIC GROUPS

These are groups like Rotary Clubs, Kiwanis Clubs, and Elks Clubs.

These groups focus on service to the community. You should join these groups because you care about your local community and not look at them as an opportunity to sell anything. While you will develop relationships within the organization and those relationships will result in business, that's not the mission of these groups, and I do not recommend you view civic groups as sales opportunities.

CHARITABLE ORGANIZATIONS

Never actively sell to someone you meet as a member of a charity. Join a charitable organization because you believe in its mission. Focus on the work the charity does. If a member of the group asks you for professional help, or inquires about your product or service, of course you can make money working with them. But a charity is not a good way to grow your business network.

EDUCATIONAL GROUPS

These are groups that help improve your professional stature. This category includes your professional trade association. If you are a lawyer, this is your local and state bar association. If you are an insurance agent, this includes the American Insurance Association and local chapters. This also includes executive educational programs – like an executive MBA or certification.

You can effectively network within these organizations if you have a niche market or subspecialty other people in your field do not focus on. For example, if you do event insurance, you can join all the insurance agent associations to network and field referrals from property and casualty agents who receive inquiries for your area of focus.

STRUCTURED NETWORKING GROUPS

These are groups that have a set system for helping members attract ideal prospects. These groups include BNI (Business Network International), LeTip International, and Leads Club. This type of group can be highly productive.

I was a member of a local BNI chapter for a number of years, and, at the most productive point in my membership, I received over $200,000 in referrals per year for a couple of years. I realize I was probably the exception to the rule, but my peers in the group received, on average, over $50,000 annually with a membership investment of less than $3,000 – including some mealtime events. That's a terrific return on investment (ROI).

These groups require a significant time commitment, and you must pass high-quality referrals to others if you want to receive high-quality referrals back.

You should explore several different types of networking groups before settling on one. Due to the amount of time and effort required, committing to multiple groups will often dilute the effectiveness of your networking capabilities. Choose carefully.

How to Make Business Networking Groups Productive

No matter what type of group you join, there is a formula to making sure you get in front of the best people in any business group. Here are the five steps to maximizing your ROI from a business networking group.

Step One: Lead or Get Out

To maximize the networking opportunity with any organization, you need to take on a leadership role. This can be as simple as joining a committee or forming a subgroup to tackle a significant challenge. Leaders build credibility and have high visibility. Find a way to lead as quickly as possible, and don't stop until you become president of the entire organization.

Step Two: Do Good and Be Seen Doing Good

Volunteer for community outreach on behalf of your organization. Take advantage of any media opportunities the organization generates. Become the group spokesperson or offer to write a column that appears in the local newspaper on behalf of the organization. Don't overtly promote your business while representing the group with the media, but do network with reporters, producers, and editors from media outlets and, when the time is right, pitch them on behalf of your business without conflicting with your group responsibilities.

Step Three: Start a Subgroup

If you belong to a large organization, it can be effective and valuable to start a subgroup based on target clientele. For example, if you are the owner of a fitness center, you can start the health and wellness sphere of your local chamber of commerce. This sphere will include nutritionists, doctors, chiropractors, physical therapists, massage therapists, and dentists, among others. This group may have similar clients and can pass referrals and organize strategic alliance partnerships.

Step Four: Become Best Friends with Professional Staff

Large groups like chambers of commerce have executive directors and membership coordinators. These people want you to be happy. They are human. Be nice to them. Make their job easy. Ask them for introductions and help when you need it. Volunteer to do all the awful jobs nobody wants to do. Endear yourself to the professional staff and they will make sure you are introduced to everyone you need to know. I cannot emphasize how important this is. The staff of every group is plugged in to everything that is happening – including community gossip that is not public yet.

Go out of your way to cultivate relationships with the people who run the organization.

STEP FIVE: RECRUIT PEOPLE INTO THE ORGANIZATION

This goes along with step four. When the group grows, the professional staff is rewarded. Help the organization grow. Volunteer to be on the membership committee or the recruiting committee. You not only help the organization grow, you will also get to meet anyone new who joins. This is your opportunity to determine if they will be a good prospective client or a potential evangelist.

Networking requires a massive time commitment. If you have the talent and desire for doing it, you must be strategic in your approach and you must go "all in." Half measures or partial efforts in networking result in total disaster. The rewards can be great, but you must be prepared to be consistent, persistent, and focused.

60 Second Actions

- ◆ Assess the amount of time you have available for networking. If you can invest the time, begin by visiting groups from the category list included in the chapter.
- ◆ When you select a networking event to attend, call the organizer and strategize in advance. Decide who you'd like to meet.
- ◆ Use the included script to begin conversations.
- ◆ Leverage the follow-up system to deepen the relationship after the initial introduction.
- ◆ If you join an organization, follow the guide to maximize the return on investment.

Chapter 12

Qualified Prospects Become Quality Clients

60 Second Summary

Most sales executives think a deal is "closed" at the end of the sales process. That's not true. In relationship-based selling, making a deal means opening a door. Anytime you talk about working together, or exchanging something of value for financial compensation, you must agree on certain rules of engagement. When the prospective client agrees to these rules, that's the "close."

The process that follows does three things:

1. Removes ambiguity from the business relationship
2. Makes the prospective client comfortable
3. Improves the likelihood you will do business with the prospective client (helps you make more deals)

What's in This Chapter for You?

You won't waste any more time in terrible meetings with prospective clients who have no money. The qualifying process is critical to your success as a relationship-based business leader because it saves you time and makes you money.

There is nothing more frustrating than sitting down with someone, having a great business meeting, and leaving the room thinking, hoping, and wishing that person would invest in a relationship with you.

The key concept you will discover in this chapter is a process to qualify everyone in advance of a business meeting. This means when you sit across from a prospect, you know he has the money to pay you, a problem you can solve, and the ability to make a decision. In other words, you're sitting across from someone who is qualified to be your client.

"Everyone" Is Not Your Client

There is a saying that goes: "Everyone needs someone to talk to." This is especially true in sales. If you are not in front of a client (physically or virtually), you are losing an opportunity to make money. This is the reason most sales managers, business leaders, and entrepreneurs reward activity.

"How many sales calls did you make this week?"

"How much time did you spend on the phone today?"

"How many people did you get in front of?"

Those are the most common ways a sales accountability conversation begins.

That's why most sales professionals fail.

That's also why so many people have negative feelings about sales and selling.

If someone is talking to you about a concept that is of no interest, and he is trying to get you to do something that never even crossed your mind, how would you feel about him?

Finding someone to talk to is not your goal. Finding the RIGHT person to talk to is the goal. When you target EVERYONE you are actually targeting no one.

Who Else Loves to Buy a Car?

Let's say you are not a "car person." You are the average parent who uses the family car to shuttle the kids to and from activities. You keep your car clean. You keep up with the maintenance schedule. You don't even think about getting a new car until the vehicle you currently drive starts to break down.

You have a perfectly good car in the driveway. It's a couple of years old but you like it. It is reliable and it is similar – almost identical – to the type of car all your friends drive.

One Tuesday evening, during dinner time, your doorbell rings. You open the door and outside is a guy in a suit. The minute you see his face, he starts talking. He immediately gives you facts and figures about the latest model vehicle from a new car company. It's called the Runzoni. The guy at the door informs you he has a Runzoni Model X out front and he wants you to test drive it, right now.

What would your reaction be?

You don't need a car. You don't have any money set aside right now to buy a car, and even if you did need a car and have the extra money lying around, you share your vehicles with your spouse so this must be a joint decision – and your spouse is finishing dinner, wondering why you are not at the table.

The door to your house would close before the plate of food on the table got cold.

Now fast-forward your thinking five years.

Your family SUV gags and coughs every time you turn off the engine. It has 145,000 miles on it, a dent in the hood from a batted baseball a couple of seasons ago, and it smells like a combination of spoiled milk and old socks. You have enough money set aside for a down payment and you've seen some ads about holiday car deals on television. You and your spouse agree it's time for a change.

You've been admiring your neighbor's luxury SUV for a while. The lift gate closes with the touch of a button, it has a lot more room than yours, and it just looks more modern and less like a rolling shoebox.

The next time you see your neighbor getting the mail, you ask him about the car. He tosses you the keys and lets you drive it. It feels good. You ask if you can have your spouse drive it. The neighbor agrees. After you go around the block a few times, you thank your neighbor and ask where he purchased the car. He gives you his salesperson's name.

You go home, swallow hard, and give the guy a call. He invites you into the car store. You and your spouse set the appointment for Saturday morning.

As you prepare for the meeting at the dealership, you visit websites and read articles about this particular car. You discover "invoice" pricing. You review the feature packages available on the car, the engine sizes, and the colors. You discuss this with your spouse. You decide what model you want, the package, the color, and the price range you can afford to pay.

You've got a knot in your stomach because you know you'll be pressured during the buying experience. You hate this process, and that's why you are driving around in the stinky shoebox SUV.

On Friday as you're walking into your home after work you see your neighbor. He waves and asks if you made an appointment to look at new cars. You share your dread with him and he gives you a brilliant idea.

"Just write down everything you want, how much you want to pay, and tell the car guy you'll come in with a check and to sign the paperwork and pick up the keys."

"Do they do it like that?" you ask.

The neighbor says: "Of course. You'd be saving him a lot of time. He knows you want a car now, you're ready to make a decision, and you have the money to buy. You're his best prospect."

So you do that. You email the sales professional. He calls you and agrees to your terms.

The meeting in the dealership takes less than 90 minutes and it only takes that long because you want to drive your new car before you sign the paperwork. The sales professional buys you a cup of coffee while they clean the car and get it ready for you to take home.

The entire experience was great – but why? Because you were a QUALIFIED buyer.

Think this never happens? Is this an unbelievable story?

Well, it's exactly how I purchased my most recent car.

If you were the sales professional in this real-life play, how can you make sure this happens EVERY TIME with EVERY PROSPECT?

That's where the qualifying process comes in.

STOP WASTING YOUR TIME TALKING TO PEOPLE WHO ARE NOT IDEAL

Throughout this book, you've discovered ideas that changed your thought process forever. This is another one of those moments.

Only work with clients who allow you to do your best work for compensation both you and your client believe is fair.

The sales process should be designed to deliver ideal clients to your doorstep. When you run clients through the qualifying process, you are checking to make sure they fit those criteria. Every minute, no, every second you spend working with or trying to attract a client who is less than ideal is wasted time.

Everyone with whom you meet must be ready, willing, and able to invest in your products and services. This means they must have a problem you can solve, money to pay you, and the ability and desire to make a decision right now.

This means they must have a problem you can solve perfectly. If you are a pharmaceutical sales representative selling a proton pump inhibitor, you must get in front of a gastroenterologist. If you are an attorney and you only handle maritime cases, you must attract clients who own seaborne vessels. If you are a veterinarian and you specialize in working with dogs, you must be in front of someone who has a dog and cares about its health.

Focus on attracting *ideal* clients, not just any client.

Money, Money, Money

If a client doesn't have money to pay you, you cannot work with him. Period.

Actually, let me clarify that statement: If a client doesn't have a fair amount of money to exchange, in return for the value you are providing, you cannot work with him. And you are the only person who determines what is *fair*.

This is a concept that is another moment of clarity for you.

You choose your clients. There are thousands of ideal people out in the world right now, looking to do business with you. You are building a process to attract them. Taking just anyone who comes along and then adapting to their conditions is a recipe for misery.

Many times, when a prospective client shows up on your doorstep, you are so excited to be meeting with someone interested in your product or service, you jump into a conversation that makes you appear needy. Instead of taking this approach, you should seek to interview the prospective client and see if he will be a good fit for a relationship with your company. This is called "qualifying the client."

You must set a minimum threshold for your compensation and make it clear to your client up front. I know you think asking for money is tough. It only seems tough because you don't have a process and a script for doing it.

A FINANCIAL ADVISOR'S SCRIPT FOR SELECTING GREAT CLIENTS

Philip is a financial advisor in Providence, Rhode Island. He makes his money in living rooms. He doesn't come to your house unless he is certain you will turn your portfolio over to him. How does he make sure you meet his minimum financial requirements?

"There are only two ways someone gets an appointment with me," says Philip.

"Either they are referred to me from a client or an evangelist or they've attended a seminar I've delivered on wealth planning and asset protection.

"Asking about money is tough, but that's my business. If I don't ask about their asset portfolio, I could end up wasting my time doing a presentation to someone who doesn't have enough money to invest."

When Philip gets a call from someone who asks for an appointment, he says:

"I am honored that you'd trust me with your retirement savings. How did you learn about me?"

If the prospective client says anything other than from a referral or from a seminar, he invites them to attend his next seminar (he runs one every month).

Next, Philip lets the prospective client know about his minimum requirement for assets under management.

"Since you attended my seminar, you know I only work with people who have $250,000 or more in investments. Are you looking to make a change with at least that amount in your portfolio?"

Then Philip asks why the timing is right to make this change now. That's his way of determining if they have a problem he can solve. He asks:

"Why is this the right time for you to move your assets? What happened that makes you want to change now?"

Finally, Philip asks the prospective client if there is anyone else who needs to be involved in this decision. He says:

"Okay, Mr. Smith. I understand you have $400,000 in your retirement account and you are unhappy with the responsiveness of your current asset manager. Is there anyone else we need to involve in this decision? The reason I ask is because, often, people make these types of decisions with a spouse or life-partner. Is there someone else we need to involve in this process?"

Once Philip has determined that the prospect has enough money, the ability to make a decision, and a problem he can solve, he outlines the ground rules for the next step in the process – a business meeting. He says:

"Mr. Smith, it looks like we have some things to talk over. The best way to do that is for the three of us – your wife, you, and me – to have a meeting.

"The purpose of this meeting is for me to understand your strategy and see if I can help you maximize your return on investment. Typically, these meetings are productive because I ask questions to determine your goals and I listen intently. You'll also have questions you want to ask and I'm happy to answer any and all of those.

"Will you invite me over to discuss this with you and your wife?"

After the meeting is set and the ground rules have been established, Philip then makes sure everyone is clear on what will happen after the meeting. Here's how Philip does it:

"When we get together, we will be evaluating each other. You're going to decide if you want to work with me and I'm going to determine if I can help you. At the end of our meeting, we will either move forward or we will part company. This means you will give me a yes or no answer on working together.

"You can ask any question you'd like. I will answer all of them. But when the meeting ends, we need to decide either yes or no on moving forward.

"Are you in agreement?"

Qualifying Process

The qualifying process consists of five steps:

> Step One: Discover if the client has a problem we can solve.
>
> Step Two: Make certain you are in front of the decision maker.
>
> Step Three: Determine if the client has the money to work with you.
>
> Step Four: Set a business meeting and lay out the ground rules.
>
> Step Five: Make sure everyone who attends the meeting is prepared to give a yes or no answer on the next step.

BREAKING DOWN THE PROCESS

Let's break down Philip's process using the five steps outlined above.

First: People know his process and his standards before they work with him. They discover them because he asks prospective clients to attend a seminar before they sit down with him for a consultation. This is important. Most financial advisors rush into the sales meeting immediately. Phillip extends the education process, so he can make sure his standards are clear at the outset. That's why he closes close to 100% of his meetings.

Since these folks attended a seminar and followed up afterward, Philip knows they have some interest in working with him. He knows they have a problem he can solve.

Second: Philip asks about making a decision in two different ways. First, he asks why the time is right to make a change now and then he asks about other people who may need to be involved in this process. By asking both of these questions Philip is making sure the prospective client knows a decision must be made and there should be nothing in the way.

Third: Philip reiterates his standards. He talks about a minimum threshold for working with him. He realizes he is in a *for-profit* business and his goal is to deliver as much value for his clients as possible in return for compensation that is commensurate with that value. He verifies they have the money to work with him.

Fourth: Philip is clear about the purpose of the meeting. He even says they will be evaluating each other. He lays out the ground rules and his expectations. This removes any ambiguity.

Finally: Philip makes sure he's going to get a decision from the client at the end of the meeting. He doesn't want the client to say "maybe" or say he "needs to think it over." Philip will risk getting a negative outcome rather than deal with the uncertainty of waiting to hear an answer later.

Set Expectations for the Prospective Client

Pay careful attention to step 5, the final step. That's the key to the entire process. If you've ever been in a great meeting and then waited for weeks expecting a decision from your prospective client, you didn't do step 5 properly.

Never, ever agree to a business meeting unless you have a promise to make a decision on whether you and the prospective client will move forward.

Somewhere in the history of sales training, somebody thought it was a good idea to disguise the purpose of the meeting. Maybe they thought it was better for the sales executive to sneak up on prospective clients and ambush them.

I don't believe in that approach.

Both you and your prospective client should arrive at a business meeting knowing there is going to be an exchange of value if conditions are optimal. This environment of transparency helps to build trust.

Here are the expectations for the meeting:

If the client believes in the value you are offering, and they trust you, they will invest in your product or service. Make sure you say this to the client before you schedule the meeting.

Getting a *no* at the end of your business meeting is fine. The timing may not be right or your solution may not be a fit. When a prospective client says "no," at least you know where you stand.

If you allow a client to say "maybe" or "let me think about it," you've put yourself in the worst possible position. You've given up control of the process.

Every business in the world should have a sign above the front door that says: "We sell things here."

Since this idea has not caught on yet, you need to gently let your prospective client know that you want money in return for the value you are providing.

Seems silly, right? It shouldn't be necessary to explain that you do this to make money.

As a consultant who solves business problems and provides sales training, I am constantly asked for free advice. The same holds true for most attorneys and accountants. Have you ever been at a group dinner with a doctor? At some point, the group will go around the table, discussing every ache and pain in the bodies of each of the attendees.

In most friendly settings, this is not an issue, but rest assured people often carry that "Can-I-just-pick-your-brain-for-a-minute?" attitude into a business meeting. You need to nip that in the bud and make it clear that you will discuss the value you provide in return for money.

That's what setting expectations in the qualifying phase is all about. Let the prospective client know you are there to establish a *for-profit* relationship.

In a business meeting, you will ask your client questions, he will ask you questions, and you will both decide if it makes sense to work together. Those are the ground rules. That's pretty simple, right?

Well, then, why do you end up leaving so many meetings wondering if and when we will do business with the client?

The answer: Because you don't discuss these ground rules in advance.

Tell the prospective client you want a yes or no answer or you're not going to meet with them. It's that simple. They can ask any questions they want. You'll stay there to answer all the questions. When those questions are finished, it's time for a decision.

LANGUAGE YOU CAN APPLY

Here are some phrases you can use as you qualify your prospective clients.

Problem You Can Solve

"What motivated you to reach out to me today?"
"What are you hoping I can do for you?"

"If you could wave a magic wand and instantly change any-thing in your life (business if you are in B-to-B sales), what would it be?"

Money

"It's my goal to help you solve this problem. That's what I do. Let's talk about the business arrangement. The minimum investment for our service is ..."

"What resources do you have to apply to this situation?"

"I'm glad you've come to me with this issue. I'd be happy to help. What is your budget for addressing this?"

Ability to Make a Decision

"Why is the timing right for solving this problem now?"

"Who else do we need to involve in this process?"

"Is there anyone else we should speak with about this deci-sion?"

"Assuming we come to an agreement, how soon can we begin our work? What or who might stand in our way?"

Ground Rules

"Here's what's going to happen when we get together."

"When you invite me over, we will be discussing your situa-tion and I'm sure you'll be asking me some questions."

"This is a meeting for us to figure out if it makes sense to work together."

Outcome

"When we finish the business meeting, we will both say either yes or no to the next step in our relationship. Are you okay with that?"

"At the end of the meeting I'd like you to be direct with me. If you don't think we should work together, will you look me in the eye and tell me? I'm an adult. I can take it. Does that make sense?"

"I don't handle 'maybe' well. Can we agree to say either yes or no at the end of the meeting?"

The Qualifying Script That Will Change Your Business Forever

Want something you can use right now? Here is a script for the entire qualifying process:

Thank you for reaching out to me. Please tell me about your situation.

How long has this been going on?

Have you consulted with another <insert your role here – consultant, attorney, accountant, car dealer, pharmaceutical executive, etc.>? If they say yes, ask: Who?

How quickly do you want to take action?

What happens if you do nothing?

Why is now the right time to do this?

Is there anyone else we need to involve in this process?

Do you consult with anyone else in your company on these types of decisions?

What financial resources do you have to apply to this situation?

Based on the situation you've outlined, it looks like I can help you. Would you like help?

Great. Let's set a time for you to invite me over to discuss things.

<Offer dates and times>

Let me describe what will happen next.

When we have our business meeting I'm going to ask you some questions, so I can fully understand your situation.

I'm sure you're going to want to ask me some questions.

I will answer all the questions you have.

After that, we will decide if it makes sense to work together.

At that point, you can say yes or you can say no.

It's really important that you agree to give a yes or no at the end of the meeting. I don't mind hearing the word no. I can handle it. Are you okay with saying no if you feel we are not a good fit?

Great.

I will see you at <DATE> <TIME>.

Now I need to be candid with you. Sometimes people schedule these appointments and they don't show up, or they cancel at the last minute. You see, they feel bad telling me they don't have the money to invest in my product/service right now.

If that's the case, please tell me.

Okay – so I can count on you to be here at <DATE> <TIME>. Right?

Did you notice the last little part I added to that script? I always let the client know that it's not acceptable to cancel a meeting. This is part of setting clear expectations. My clients and I are peers, we're partners in this relationship. People who are partners are candid and direct.

Besides, cancellations and no shows are terrible and unprofessional.

There's nothing worse than flying cross-country on a Sunday night to attend a meeting early Monday morning, only to find out the person with whom you are meeting has "a conflict."

THE ORIENTATION PACKET

There is a powerful tool you must include in your sales cycle. This tool is called the *orientation packet*. Here's how it works.

After the qualifying call where you set an appointment and before you meet with the client, you send a physical packet of information designed to introduce you, promote you, and help the client see what makes you different from everyone else who does what you do. This orientation packet is a physical folder or, in some cases, a binder full of information. The packet contains five things:

1. *Cover letter with your bio:* This is a simple letter in which you introduce yourself to the client in a formal way. You explain what is included in the packet and you attach your biographical sketch (your bio). Your bio should be a short narrative detailing what you've done during your career. This is similar to your career summary on LinkedIn.

2. *Your honeypot:* It never hurts to make sure the client understands one of the most pressing problems facing the industry today. Your honeypot addresses that problem. In addition, if you've created any other reports that you've used as honeypots, you include those as well. Remember: The way you write is the way you think. Demonstrate your clear, logical thinking by sending those reports.

3. *Reprints of published articles:* Include authorized reprints of any published articles you've written. This enhances your credibility. It doesn't matter if the articles are related to the work you will be doing for the prospective client. What we are after is the impact the article being published will have on the client's perception of you.

4. *Testimonials:* These are key. Include every testimonial letter anyone has ever written for you. If they have given you audio or video testimonials, have them transcribed and put the transcript with the identifying information of the person quoted in the packet. The idea is to create a "preponderance of evidence" that you are the best possible person to work with.

5. *Meeting agenda:* This item is important. This is a document that outlines how the business meeting will proceed and what the next steps will be after the meeting. This document assumes you will work with the client after the meeting.

Your goal is to get the orientation packet to the client before the meeting with you. If possible, send the orientation packet via overnight express mail. This will make a positive impression and it conveys how serious you are about your business and the value you provide to your clients.

Note: Do not try to save money by emailing these documents to the prospective client. This is not the time to be cheap. The physical presentation is just as important as the information in the packet. The folder or binder should be impressive. The documents should be printed on high-quality paper. Any article reprints should be color, glossy prints with the publication's banner on the top of the article page.

60 Second Actions

◆ Review the results of your IRT 21 interview (Chapter 4) again and confirm your ideal client's profile. See if you've added any new clients since you last completed an IRT 21 interview. Your ideal client may have changed. Make sure you're still targeting the right type of prospect.

◆ Review the qualifying steps and customize them to fit your business.

◆ Write out an actual qualifying script you can use. Practice it and modify the language as needed.

◆ Immediately incorporate the qualifying script into your sales process. Review it with your team and train them on it.

◆ Put together an orientation packet and have the five components ready to send to prospects with whom you will be meeting.

Chapter 13

Open a Door and Close the Deal

60 Second Summary

This chapter highlights the process of converting the prospect into a client. You do this by continuing the running conversation you've had with them since they were first introduced to you.

Since the client walks into the room ready to do business, your job is to not screw that up. Let that sink in for a minute.

Fear not. I've choreographed the entire meeting for you. That choreography is outlined in this chapter.

What's in This Chapter for You?

This is your guide to the business meeting when you discuss the value the client will receive and the money they will pay.

This is a delicate conversation, and many bad things can happen if it isn't handled properly. In this chapter, I take you by the hand and lead you through how this meeting will work when done properly.

The key concept you will discover in this chapter is offering the client options for working with you. *Yes or no* sales is dead. Moving forward, you will only provide prospective clients with *yes* options. This is the most powerful way to increase your income. It also helps reduce the likelihood of negotiation.

WNABE™

The old sales adage "Always Be Closing" is no longer appropriate. Getting in someone's face and pushing your product or service on them is the fastest way to turn people off. Sales has changed. You've been investing in relationships, and the time has come to help people solve their problems and achieve their goals.

Now that you've been invited in to a business meeting to have a serious discussion, you need a framework. That framework is called WNABE™.

WNABE™ is an acronym. Here's what it stands for:

- ◆ Uncover what the prospective client **W**ANTS.
- ◆ Focus on what the prospective client actually **N**EEDS.
- ◆ Determine what the prospective client is going out of his way to **A**VOID.
- ◆ Demonstrate how your product or service will **B**ENEFIT the prospective client.
- ◆ Increase the prospective client's **E**MOTIONAL engagement toward your solution.

As the meeting begins, you want to confirm the agenda with your prospective client. This is an important step, because you must be clear about the focus of your time together. Here is the script you should use to confirm the agenda:

It is great to see you today. I'm looking forward to our conversation. Before we get into the details, let's review our agenda.

You will be telling me about your situation – your goals – what you are hoping we can accomplish together. I'm going to ask you some questions, so I can fully understand your situation.

I'm sure you're going to want to ask me some questions. I will answer all the questions you have.

Then we will discuss whether or not we should work together. If working together makes sense, we'll discuss the options for that. If it doesn't, we will part company as friends.

At that point, you can say *yes* or you can say *no* to a working relationship.

I don't mind hearing the word *no*. I can handle it.

Are you okay with our agenda?

Once you have agreement on the agenda, then you can get into the first part of the WNABE™ process.

UNCOVER WHAT THE PROSPECT **WANTS**

You start the conversation by asking, "What brings you here today?" Then you shut up. Don't say anything. You might want to take some notes, but it is more important that you listen.

What you will hear during this part of the meeting is probably not the actual problem. What you are going to hear are symptoms of the problem. These are the things that are bothering the client or the concerns the client has about the issue. But they are not the issue itself.

Here is an example from one of my client's business conversations. My client is a financial advisor and he is sitting with a corporate executive, who says the following:

> "I'm not sure I'm going to be able to fund college for my children. They are 5 and 7 years old. I only have 10 years, and the cost of school is going up rapidly each year. I haven't started saving yet. I make good money, but I don't know how much I can save. It seems after I pay the bills, there's never any money left over each month. I'm really worried about this. I think about it all the time."

The problem is not funding college. It is the lack of a financial plan and the discipline to execute that plan.

In this case, the corporate executive doesn't come in looking for a plan and discipline. He wants to be able to sleep at night.

FOCUS ON WHAT THE PROSPECT ACTUALLY **NEEDS**

Usually, within two or three minutes of beginning a conversation with the prospect, you'll know what he needs. This is what you've been doing as a career and you've seen quite a bit. But you need to let the prospect say everything there is to say. Let him get everything off his chest.

When there is a break in the conversation, ask questions that get to the heart of the matter. Explore what is behind the client's words. Ask questions and say things like:

- "I understand everything you're saying. Tell me where these concerns are coming from."
- "What you're describing is a concern. I see that. What's driving this?"
- "Everything you're saying makes perfect sense to me. What is behind this?"
- "What is the source of these issues? Is there something happening below the surface driving this?"
- "Tell me more about the things you believe are driving these issues. Are we discussing symptoms or the actual issue?"

Now, maybe for the first time, the prospect will get to the core of the issue. That's when you can begin to formulate what the prospect actually needs.

Keep in mind, you MUST draw this out. The prospect himself must come to the realization of the actual problem. You can't reveal it to him. If you immediately announce the problem, based upon your experience, there is a high likelihood the prospect will resent you. That's human nature. If you say what the problem is, the prospect will project the problem onto you and will run away from you as fast as possible.

What Is the Prospect AVOIDING?

Next, you must uncover what they are trying to avoid. There is a reason the prospective client has not solved this problem (or achieved this goal) yet. There is a risk in taking the step toward a solution. Here are some questions you can ask to uncover what risk the prospect is avoiding:

- "Why haven't you solved this problem yet?"
- "What has been holding you back?"
- "Is there something keeping you from taking action?"
- "What could possibly give you some relief? Why aren't you experiencing that now?"

◆ "If you had unlimited resources, how quickly could you get to a solution? What would that look like? Why not do that?"

The reason you are asking these questions is to assess the risks that prospective client sees that might prevent him from doing business with you. There are seven types of risk clients face when they enter into a business relationship.

Risk of Physical Harm This risk is not one most people will be concerned about. If you work in the health and wellness industry, your prospective clients may be concerned about the side effects of taking a supplement or a medication. They may worry about physical discomfort associated with therapy or with beginning a workout program.

You help the prospect overcome concern about this by having a well-defined process for delivering your product and/or service. You also should have some successful clients available for the prospect to connect with.

Risk of Poor Performance This is not the risk that you or your product won't perform. This is the risk that your solution won't work for this specific client.

Again, think back to the doctor analogy. Every treatment prescribed has a small-percentage probability of being ineffective, yet we all go into it thinking we could be in that minority.

Whenever I deliver sales training to a company, the CEO asks: "What if my people just don't respond? We've done training here before and the folks just didn't use it. What are the chances of that happening?" That CEO is concerned about the performance of his people.

The most effective way to overcome this is with an actual case study. Detail the results someone else, in a similar business, received after having this exact concern.

You should also mention that the buy-in from the team is directly related to the commitment of the leadership. If the leaders are not 100% convinced that this solution will work, it will fail.

Financial Risk Nobody wants to waste money. You need to demonstrate a return on investment for the product or service you provide. At minimum, you should demonstrate how the client will receive a return that meets his expectations. There are ways to get to the heart of this issue. The easiest is with a seemingly innocent question while the client is telling their story. Ask:

- "What do you think this is costing you?"
- "That sounds expensive. Is it?"
- "If you could put a number on the cost of this issue, what would it be? Just guess."

After they give you that number, you need to build your case for a return on investment that exceeds that number.

Risk of Lost Time Nobody wants to waste time. The best way to approach this is to turn it around on the person who is asking about it. When the prospect says, "If this doesn't work, I will have wasted all that time!" You say, "You're wasting time right now by not implementing a solution. Why do you want to wait any longer?"

Risk of Lost Opportunity This is only an issue if the prospective clients knew of another solution they could be using instead of yours. If they do, and they raise this as an issue, you simply use the same strategy as with lost time – you turn it around on them.

"You're concerned about another solution when you have not even given ours a chance yet. Remember your commitment is key to making this work. If you want to try another solution first, go ahead. I don't want you going into this with any doubt."

That type of strong response enhances your credibility. It demonstrates confidence.

Psychological Risk This is the concern that the product or service will not fit who the client is as a person. This is completely embedded in their psyche. It's the reason people drive expensive cars. It is the reason people stay in luxury hotels. It is the reason people dress well. They do those things because they reinforce the image they have of themselves.

If this is an issue, make sure you highlight some "famous" or "prestigious" people who have worked with you in the past.

Social Risks This is the risk of a negative opinion in the mind of your prospective client's friends or industry associates when they see them with you or your product. It is important to build your client up as an industry or community leader. This will help insulate them from these concerns. Express to them the need for "being a pioneer" and "charting new territory" and "setting the standard for the industry."

DEMONSTRATE HOW YOUR PRODUCT OR SERVICE WILL **BENEFIT** THE PROSPECTIVE CLIENT

You are now at the part of the meeting where you introduce the solution to your prospective client. You do not introduce the solution in a vacuum. You don't just say, "Here is how we solve your problem," or "Here's how we help you achieve your goal."

You frame the benefits of working with you within the context of the information the prospect has already shared.

Since the prospect has powerfully articulated the symptoms, you are going to articulate the solution using those exact words. It is only after you discuss how you are going to relieve the symptoms that you can discuss the solution you will provide to the problem. That's because the prospective client is concerned about the immediate pain.

Using the financial advisor example:

"You are concerned about paying for college for your kids. As long as we start now, you have plenty of time. What we need to do is sit down and talk about your income, your expenses, and then formulate a plan to make sure the money is there when you and your kids need it. After we get the plan together, we will set up automatic investments you don't even have to think about. I will monitor those investments for you and we can meet as often as you'd like to discuss them. This way, you can sleep at night and you have a professional keeping an eye on the kids' college fund."

In defining the benefits, we focused on the symptoms yet addressed the problem in a comprehensive way.

INCREASE THE PROSPECTIVE CLIENT'S EMOTIONAL ENGAGEMENT TOWARD YOUR SOLUTION

The final aspect of the WNABE™ process is to increase the prospective client's **E**MOTIONAL engagement toward your solution.

This means you want the prospective client fully committed to the solution you've designed. The best way to do this is to get the client to articulate how things will improve once you've completed your work together.

Say: "Think about what things will look like when this problem is solved. How will you feel? What difference will it make to your life? How will solving this problem impact you personally?"

Do not let the client off the hook with this. You need to hear an emotional answer. You want the client to mentally enter a time and place when the problem is solved.

Time to Talk about Money

Nobody likes yes or no choices when buying something. As a business leader, you should hate those binary choices as well. They limit the amount of money you can make to your best guess on the client's budget. Of course, you can ask the clients what they have in the budget for your product or service, but they aren't going to be honest with you. Besides, you should decide how much your product or service is worth based upon the value you are providing.

Since you've worked the 60 Second Sale system to this point, you have put yourself in a position to discuss value and investment.

Notice the language there. We are not using words like *fees*, *charges*, or *bills*. Your clients are receiving value from you for an investment they are making. Use the language and make the mind-set shift.

HOW TO IDENTIFY AND COMMUNICATE VALUE

You are underestimating the value you provide to your clients. We all do. That's why I've created a guide you can use to assess the value you are providing BEFORE you come up with a price for your product or service.

Area of Impact: Strengthen the Client's Situation

1. *Reducing risk:* We've already discussed risk in this chapter within the context of the clients making a decision. Now think about it as it relates to their business. Can you help them reduce the seven elements of risk?

2. *Facilitating an outcome:* Can you help a client make something happen? This might mean achieving a goal or gaining an advantage.

3. *Preventing an adverse consequence:* Do you have the ability to stop something bad from happening to the client? Are you uniquely suited to clear up a damaging claim?

4. *Delaying adversity:* Can you delay the inevitable? Do you have the ability to help clients buy time and assess options?

5. *Confirming hypothesis, providing comfort:* Are you able to assess a situation and provide guidance or support? Can you confirm or disprove assumptions?

These five areas of impact can dramatically increase the client's perception of your value. Make sure you give them serious consideration before developing a proposal.

Area of Impact: Your Personal Differentiating Factors

1. *Talent (natural, inborn, gifts):* Are you naturally great at something? Some people can sing and some people can't. Are you naturally great with numbers? Are you an outstanding wordsmith? Do your clients have access to you for those talents?

2. *Skills (learned through training and experience):* Do you bring something to a client organization that is difficult to find anywhere else?

3. *Knowledge (acquired through study):* Can you level out the learning curve for your clients? Can you serve as a shortcut for them in some area?

4. *The Experience (your "bedside manner"):* This is how the client feels working with you. Are your clients happy to see you? Is the way you work enjoyable to the clients? Are you fun to be around?

5. *Results (documented positive outcomes you've achieved for clients in the past):* What is your track record? Can you demonstrate success under difficult conditions?

6. *Work Product (peer review as well as client opinion):* Is your work product consistently outstanding? Can you provide examples as well as reviews or assessments of your work?

7. *Service (speed of return calls, adherence to nonbinding deadlines):* Are you client-focused in every way? Do clients routinely remark about the way you go about your business?

These seven areas are specific to you and your company. Be sure to highlight each one of them that you feel is an advantage. These are valuable to your client.

Area of Impact: Urgency   What is the client's level of urgency? Can you accommodate it?

1. *Immediate action required:* Is there a burning platform? If so, this is a value multiplier – meaning you can command an investment premium because you have to drop everything.

2. *Pressing need:* Time is of the essence, so you need to move, but you can create a plan and take measured action.

3. *Important:* Your work is important to the client

OPTIONS, OPTIONS, OPTIONS

Once you assess each of these areas of impact, you can create a proposal. This is where the magic comes in. You do not ever, under any circumstance, offer just a *yes or no* option. Instead you offer a "good," "better," "best" selection of options.

Here's how this works:

◆ *Good option:* This is exactly what the client wants and needs. It helps the client achieve the goal and/or solve the problem. You demonstrate the return on investment. You demonstrate how this strengthens a client's situation. You demonstrate your personal differentiating factor. You demonstrate how you can meet the client's level of urgency.

◆ *Better option:* You do everything as listed in the good option, plus you go the extra mile and help prevent this situation from recurring, or you help ensure an ongoing revenue stream, or you provide an unexpected but suddenly necessary service based on your due diligence. Financially, the investment for this option starts at 75% more than the good option (but can be multiples of it).

◆ *Best option:* You do everything as listed in both options above and also help actively transform the client's business to take it to a different level and help the client achieve a personal goal. Financially, the investment for this option starts at 100% more than the good option.

We have seen options used as value leverage in product sales for years. The most common product with a plethora of options is automobile sales. There are trim option packages, color options, and performance options. It is easy to offer choices with products based on their design. I urge you to consider the areas of impact I've listed and use them as leverage to enhance your relationship with your client when selling products. As we have discussed, you sell yourself and you sell the client on a relationship with you, above and beyond the value the product will deliver to the client. Consider the factors in the areas of impact and craft options that include both product options and options specific to you and your relationship with the client.

Here are some service examples:

Pool Design and Construction Business

Primary Design and Construction Service: Pool design and construction based on selection of one of our template designs with no customization. You choose from our basic pool deck surfaces and our concrete liner options. Construction begins within 30 days of final payment and is complete within 90 days. We guarantee workmanship and materials for 3 years and will replace anything that breaks at our expense during that time regardless of the reason, no exceptions. Investment = $100,000.

VIP Design and Construction Service: This upgraded level of design and construction includes a customized design of your pool, choice of premium deck surface material, and upgraded liner options. Construction begins within 10 days of final payment and is complete within 60 days. We guarantee workmanship and material for 10 years and will replace anything that breaks at our expense during that time regardless of reason, no exceptions. Investment = $250,000.

Elite Design and Construction Service: This upgraded level of design and construction includes a unique design of your pool by our award-winning designer, choice of premium deck surface material, and highest-quality liner options. Construction begins the day of final payment and is complete within 45 days, even if we have to work double shifts. We guarantee workmanship and material for the duration of your ownership of the home and will replace anything that breaks at our expense during that time, regardless of reason, no exceptions. In addition, we will provide an annual deep cleaning of the pool surface and tile, and upon request, we will inspect and replace all valves, seals, and piping each year to ensure optimal operation. Investment = $350,000.

The pool design example is one that can be used as a reference for architects, construction sales professionals, landscape designers, and anyone in a service and materials business.

When it comes to professionals like attorneys, CPAs, and other people who usually bill by the hour, we need to craft an offer that uses access to the professional to provide additional value:

Law Firm, CPA Firm, or Consulting Firm
One of the things that makes our firm different is the investment choices we offer our clients.

[If client says something about the word *investment*:]

We use that term because you are investing in the future of your business. Our work together will <allow you to make a fresh start> <help you to put this issue behind you> <help you resolve this dispute>. We approach relationships with our clients from this perspective. We know this is critically important to you and your future.

There are three ways we can approach our work together:

The **first** way is for us to do a comprehensive assessment of your situation at the outset. We examine all aspects of your business and we present you with an objective analysis of the issue you are facing. We find that sometimes clients don't have a sense of the depth of their issues or of all their options when they come to us.

After we complete the strategic review, we will then be able to offer you one investment for the remainder of our services on this matter. There will be no meter running. As long as the scope of our work doesn't change, you can call us as often as you'd like without any additional bills being sent to you.

The investment for the strategic review is $xx,000. After the review is complete, we will discuss the investment for the remainder of our work.

The **second** way for us to work together is to segment our work and apply investment options to each segment. This provides you with budgeting flexibility.

In your case, segment one would include all work up to …
Segment two includes …
Segment three includes …

While we've found this option to be convenient for budgeting purposes, in most cases, it is not as cost-effective as the upfront assessment and flat fee.

The **final** option for investing in our work together is the standard professional/client investment relationship. We align our goals with yours, and our team works aggressively to resolve your situation. Each of the members of our firm keeps a record of time spent and we provide you with an invoice each month reflective of the actual work done to advance your case toward resolution.

This method requires a minimum retainer of $XX,000, and that is used as a deposit and applied toward the final invoice.

The hourly rates of our team members are reflective of their experience, knowledge, and strengths.

Ultimately, the choice is yours.

Clients have told us they prefer option one because of the certainty.

I hate hourly billing, but if we don't include an hourly billing option for professionals, especially attorneys, I receive a significant number of complaints. There is not enough room within these pages for us to discuss and debate this subject.

60 Second Actions

◆ Think about your ideal client relationship and assess it through the lens of the WNABE™ framework. Knowing what you know now, outline how you would address the client's issues as if they were a prospect in a WNABE™ meeting today. Write out how that meeting would proceed. Prepare an actual outline as if you are having that discussion with a client.

◆ Bring in a team member and rehearse the WNABE™ process based on the outline above. Practice this several times so it becomes natural.

◆ Use the same method to create options for your best client based on your intimate knowledge of their business.

◆ Rehearse delivering these options to a team member so you can deliver them in your next client presentation.

◆ Review both of these processes with an actual client. Get feedback. Modify as necessary.

Chapter 14

The End of the Beginning

We have covered a lot of information in the 60 Second Sale system. It probably seems overwhelming. That's why I'm going to give you some specific next steps to follow, and I'm going to prioritize them based on how far along you are in your evolution from hit-and-run sales to relationship-based sales.

Harsh Reality

Congratulations on getting to this chapter in this book. You are special. Since you've come this far, I'm hoping you will go a little further. Based on my experience with sales executives, business leaders, professionals, and entrepreneurs, here are the categories of people who will move forward beyond this point.

The bottom 20% do NOTHING. They purchased the book. They may have skimmed it. They stumbled upon this page but they will not take action. They want to take action. At some point in the future they may find this book in their bookcase, or propping open a window somewhere, and decide to dig in and get to work. I welcome that.

The next 30% do one thing. They found something in the book that is the breakthrough they have been looking for. This breakthrough will immediately boost their sales. They will work on this specific activity until they have it down cold. This person will write me a great book review and I will be forever grateful.

The next 30% read the entire book and pick out three or four activities to begin immediately. In fact, they started some of them while they were reading. People in this category are telling their friends how excited they are for their future. They recommend the book to a coworker. This book sits atop their desk and they keep leafing back and forth to the scripts, checklists, and templates.

The next 15% read the book quickly and have already planned out all the actions they will take. They went to the website with the video course http://DoThisSellMore.com and signed up. They have two copies of the book – one on their nightstand at home and one on their desk. Both of these books have notes and are highlighted. Each time these folks read the book, they pick up on something new they missed the last time. Some of these people call me and accuse me of having written different versions of the book.

The next 4% are truly students of the 60 Second Sale system. They do everything described above and, in addition, they truly get "inside the mind of their client." They focus on building relationships and driving client lifetime value. They track and measure everything. They have set up systems for everything we've discussed in the book. They have modified some of the ideas to fit their industry, company, and strengths.

The top 1% do all of the above but do it obsessively, and if they don't know how to do something they find out how to do it. They go the extra mile with their personal growth and education. They constantly test new tactics. They avail themselves of every educational opportunity, and they have the attitude that they only need to learn and implement *one* idea from a seminar or coaching program and it will pay for itself several times over.

If you are one of these people in the top 1%, I have an elite mentoring program for you. There is a significant investment, but the return on that investment will change your career. Call my office for an application: 888.444.5150.

Since you've read all the categories of people who have made it to this point in the book, and you have mentally slotted yourself in one of them, I'm going to list 20 possible next steps for you. Based upon your self-evaluation, act accordingly.

Action Checklist

◆ Each day, send a handwritten thank you note to one evangelist and one client.

◆ Each day, use the script in Chapter 2 to start a conversation with a complete stranger. Eventually it will get easier, but you must do it.

◆ Set up your natural network in a spreadsheet.

◆ Import that spreadsheet into a CRM software system.

◆ Call people in your natural network and reconnect with them.

◆ Send everyone in your natural network an email reconnecting.

◆ Send everyone in your natural network a physical letter.

◆ Repeat the natural network activities as listed above at least twice more.

◆ Interview your best clients using the IRT 21 interview.

◆ Begin writing a weekly email newsletter. Send it out on the same day and time each week.

◆ Begin writing a monthly newsletter. Mail it once each month.

◆ Create a primary internet presence.

◆ Add the articles you write to the article section of the website.

◆ Create a honeypot.

◆ Set up automated delivery of your honeypot through your email or CRM system.

◆ Using the results of your IRT 21 interview, find groups to whom you can deliver speeches.

◆ Using the results of your IRT 21 interview find publications to which you can pitch articles.

◆ Set up a YouTube channel. Begin recording and uploading at least two videos each week.

◆ Review networking groups in your area. Check out one new group each month. Only join if you think there is value.

◆ Experiment with internet advertising. Use your IRT 21 interview results to target websites your ideal clients visit. Invest small money at first and only go big if the return is evident.

Just Do One Thing

This is a checklist of the 20 things you can do to get off to a fast start. Pick one of them and do it. Then come back tomorrow and pick another one. If you find one of them is particularly easy, and you enjoy it, and you get great results, keep doing that until you get sick of it. Then assign it to someone else and start another one.

That's a key point.

You might get bored with one of the activities in the 60 Second Sale system at some point. That's normal. DO NOT STOP when you get bored. Simply assign the activity to someone else or hire someone to do it. Stopping is bad. Assigning it to someone is fine. Keep the momentum going.

Confused, Stuck, or Have an Idea?

Many of the concepts in this book were refined over years and years of trial and error. I'm grateful to the hundreds of clients who helped me make them work. If you have evidence of how you've successfully modified an aspect of the 60 Second Sale system, I'd love to hear about it.

Use the form on the website for the video course: http://DoThisSellMore.com to tell me all about it.

Each year I convene a meeting of outstanding sales professionals and entrepreneurs from all over the world. This is called the Strategic Sales Academy. I invite people who use the 60 Second Sale system to share their success with the audience. I'm looking forward to seeing you up on stage with me sharing your knowledge with the best and the brightest relationship-based business leaders!

Parting Shots: Seven Mistakes Sales Leaders Make

An Open Letter to a Sales Manager

Dear Sam Salesboss,

As much as I hate to admit it, I need you. You are essential to my success. Too often you do things that screw everything up. There are many reasons for this.

One is because you didn't get enough training before they put you in this job.

Another is because you were a great salesperson and they made you a manager. Selling is in your DNA. You can't help yourself. You have your style and I have mine. Neither is wrong or right. But we are different.

Yet another reason is because the folks at corporate don't really understand what happens "out in the field" and you're stuck in the middle.

But the bottom line is that we need each other. If I exceed my sales goals, I make more money and you get credit for being a great boss. So here are seven areas where many sales managers in the past have screwed things up.

I share these with you so we can both be successful. Read them. Think about them. Then put yourself in my shoes and do whatever you think is right.

Seven Mistakes Sales Leaders Make That Screw Everything Up

MISTAKE 1: NOT LOOKING OUT FOR MY WALLET

The most important thing for me is getting paid. I want to help my clients and be fairly compensated for doing it. I make sure the client pays on time, sometimes early, sometimes even up front. Your most important job is making sure I get paid on time.

The company will want to change the way I get paid or how much I get paid. Please fight for my compensation to be the same as it was when I was hired. I like selling at this company. I agreed to the deal we have now. If I blow the doors off the compensation, don't let them change it.

Mistake 2: Guarding Sales Territories Like They Are Your Grandmother's Pearls

Sales territories are stupid. If I live in New York and my college roommate is now CEO of a company in Phoenix, let me sell to him. This is good for the client (he will get great service), it's good for our company (because I will close a deal with a company nobody else was thinking about calling on), and it's good for me and you (because we will make money).

Let me call on anyone I want as long as I represent the company with honor and integrity and I put the best interest of the client before anything else. I have sales radar, and sometimes my client relationships will take me two counties, two states, or two countries away from my territory. Let me go get those clients. I'll come home a winner.

Mistake 3: Pestering Me for Paperwork

If you want reports, hire accountants. If you want money in the bank, I'm the person for you. If I make only 10 sales calls each year and produce $10 million in business, would you get on me for not making enough calls?

Focus on results and not on paperwork.

Mistake 4: Promoting Yourself to My Clients

Sometimes we will meet with my clients together. I don't like this, but if it needs to happen, so be it. When you and I are together with my clients, you need to make me look good. Or at least not make me look bad.

One of the worst things you can do is tell stories about yourself. Your glory days are not important to my client. They are not important to me, either, but I put up with those stories around the office because, well, you are the boss.

Save your war stories for barbecues at your house.

Mistake 5: Taking Pleasure in My Failure

Sometimes I will be rejected. That sucks. You know how much that sucks. Help me through those difficult times. Remind me that my next win is right around the corner. Encourage me to make another call, send another email, schedule another meeting.

Your encouragement is valuable and much appreciated.

Mistake 6: Loving Me When I'm Winning; Hating Me When I'm in a Slump

Remember my track record. I'm the same person whether I'm on the top of the leaderboard or in a deep, deep slump. Please don't treat me differently. I put enough pressure on myself, and I don't need any additional pressure.

When I get home, my family will ask me if I sold anything today. That is enough pressure. I'm still the person who was on top of the board a few months ago. I'll be up there again. Treat me the same either way.

Mistake 7: Trying to Make Me a Manager

I love selling. I love my clients. I love delivering value to clients and getting paid to do it. Don't make me a manager. I have a healthy ego. That works for a sales executive. It doesn't work for a manager.

I like having unlimited income opportunity. Leave me alone and let me sell. I will make you look good and make a great living doing it.

Mr. Salesboss, I want you to be successful. I want the company to be successful. If you review these seven areas and take my advice, we will all do well together.

Thank you for everything you do, and thanks for letting me do what I do.

Regards,
Tommy Topproducer

Glossary

David Mamet, the American playwright and author, is fantastic at writing dialogue for characters in his books, plays, and movies. The characters are speaking English, but they seem to bend the language to their will.

This is also true in sales.

While I fall far short of Mamet's literary brilliance, I have "bent" a word or two in the 60 Second Sale system. For that reason, I have included a glossary here. If you want to know what these words and phrases mean in real life, use a dictionary. When you're working with me, I want us to speak the same language.

ACTION™ advertising This is an acronym that stands for:

    Attract attention.

    Captivate the audience.

    Tempt the audience to make a decision.

    Inform the audience what will happen if they don't act now.

    Offer them something.

    Nurture them after they've taken action.

Ad hoc income This is transactional revenue. Sell and move on.

Belly-to-belly One-on-one sales, face-to-face.

Business meeting This is when you get together with a prospective client and discuss their needs, problems, and goals. This is also where you share your ideas for helping the client. The goal of a business meeting is to come to an agreement on an exchange of value. It's where you have the closing conversation.

Charitable organizations These groups exist to fulfill a mission. The focus is to raise funds and help a specific group or cause.

Civic groups These are organizations designed to help the community. Their primary purpose is to enrich the geographic area they serve.

Clarity of purpose When you know exactly why you are doing something. You have the outcome in mind the entire time. For example: When you give a speech, your clarity of purpose is to get the contact information from everyone in the room so you can send them a honeypot.

Client trade associations Groups of people, some of whom are your clients, who work in the same profession.

Client vs. customer A client is someone who buys from an individual. A customer is someone who buys from a business. Calling someone a client indicates a relationship and calling someone a customer is indicative of a transactional approach. In our work together, you and I focus on relationships. That's why we have clients.

CRM Acronym for client relationship management system. This is software to help you manage your contact database.

Database This is your list of contacts and all the information and notes it contains about each of your relationships.

Dumb money ad An advertisement run for product-recognition purposes.

Educational groups These are organizations designed for individual intellectual enrichment and continuing personal growth.

Evangelist Someone who refers business to you even though he or she has never used your product or service.

Exchange of value You agree to help a client solve a problem or achieve a goal in return for financial compensation. This could mean selling the client a product or service for a fee, or it could also mean providing a unique experience in return for financial compensation.

External orientation Placing the benefit of others as the primary objective in your interaction.

FOMO An acronym that stands for *fear of missing out*. Motivating factor used to get people to take action.

Frat boy approach Asking people to do business with you having never met them or even had a conversation with them.

General business groups These are community-based business organizations and chambers of commerce.

Ground rules The rules under which you and the prospect will have a business meeting. The phrase comes from baseball. Each park where teams play is different and has special nuances. When a new team comes into town, the umpire reviews the ground rules with both teams. He does this so things are transparent and fair. The ground rules in the business meeting exist for the same reason.

Hit-and-run sales This is old-school selling. You cold call, stick your foot in the door, sell the product or service any way you can, and then move on without regard for relationships.

Honeypot This is an engagement device you use to attract the interest of suspects and convert them into prospects. Free reports make excellent honeypots because they can be tailored to the specific audience and delivery system.

IRT 21 Ideal Relationship Targeting 21. The 21 questions you can use to uncover how to target your ideal client, develop the appropriate message for them, and select the correct delivery systems to use to reach them.

MAD Three-letter acronym to help in developing relationships: Message, Audience, Delivery system.

Natural network Everyone you know. The people you come into contact with as you go about your daily life. People you've met in the various roles you've held in your career.

Old-school sales Cold calling, product/service focused sales. Pitching vs. listening.

Orientation packet This is a folder full or information designed to help prepare your client for a meeting with you. It contains five things: a cover letter, bio, your honeypot, reprints of articles you've written, and an agenda for the meeting with you.

Primary internet presence A website with great content to help people get to know you. Everyone needs one. Even if your company has a website, you must have your own personal website.

Prospect (short for prospective client) Someone who has reached out in some way and shown an interest in you, your business, and the value you provide.

RaporMax® System This is your primary sales operating system. Everyone you've ever met and everyone you will meet is immediately entered into it. You start it up with people in your natural network and it grows over time. This system is the key to closing deals, deepening relationships, and skyrocketing lifetime value.

Recurring income This is revenue from the same activity done over and over again.

Relationship income Unsolicited, passive income from people in your network.

Relationship Report Card™ score A leading indicator of the strength of a relationship between you and a client. A higher score is indicative of a stronger relationship.

Repeat income This is revenue developed from contact you initiate. The revenue is generated from sale of a product or service the client has not previously purchased from you.

Structured networking groups Business groups with a process for generating and passing referrals among members.

Suspect A person you believe has the qualities of your best clients.

Testimonial An endorsement of your work by someone who has no financial interest in your success.

Acknowledgments

There would be no *60 Second Sale* without Shannon Vargo, associate publisher at John Wiley & Sons. Thank you for your trust.

Special thanks to Kelly Martin at Wiley for keeping things on track and answering dozens of stupid questions.

Thank you to Steve Carlis and Hank Norman at 2 Market Media for your guidance, support, and effort on my behalf.

There are some people to whom I will never be able to adequately express my gratitude. They include:

My wife, my best friend, and the person with the best laugh on Earth, Kary Cheda.

My children, Nicholas and Dahlia. You make me proud every day, and I'm lucky to be your dad.

My kids before I had kids, Angela and Angelica. I was lucky you came into my life when you did, and I'm even luckier to have you in my life as you become adults.

My sister, Laura, for her unconditional love.

My parents, Vince and Rosemary, for their love, sacrifice, and endless hours of worry.

My two other sisters, Josephine and Kat, who I got as part of the best package deal in history.

Maria and Manny Lorenzo, with whom we've shared the best memories of the past 12 years and with whom we will share many more.

The clients who have been with me from the beginning and are still with me today: Patrick D. Murphy of North Conway, New Hampshire, Bradley Gross, Marla Porter-Gross, Steven Klitzner, and Russell Jacobs.

Thanks also to my good friend, Geoff Brewer. Every conversation I have with you makes me laugh and makes me smarter.

Special thanks to Brian Tannebaum. I'm a Jets fan. I sell things to lawyers. I could not be more ignorant about wine. And I'd rather listen to Van Halen than Sade. I'm not sure how we hit it off, but somehow we became friends, and I'm glad we did.

Finally, thanks to the guy who really can sell anything: Patrick J. Murphy – originally from North Salem, New York. Pat is a guy who can sell paper in a digital age, which makes him an exceptional sales professional. But more importantly, Pat is a guy who can remain friends with an anxious, impulsive, sometimes cranky agoraphobe who never knows how to wear his hair – across the miles and through the years. For this, I will always be grateful.

My life has been full of colorful characters. I'm grateful for having met all of them. These pages are not of sufficient heft to contain all those stories, but they all live on in my memory.

I share those stories with my children, but the ones that stand out most prominently now, because of the age of my kids, are the Friday nights on 90th Street in Howard Beach. Von Algenon, cheesecake, and pastina. The Yankees on a black and white TV, and crossword puzzles. Atari. Star Trek. The screened-in porch. And the smell of pork chops. The first signed copy of this book goes to Aunt Ter, with lots of love.

Regards, Nettie. Regards.

About the Author

This part of the book is supposed to be written in the third person, but since I've written this entire book as a conversation, I figured it didn't make much sense to change things now.

You already know a lot about my career, but I'll fill in a couple of the details for you.

I grew up working in an Italian restaurant and a supermarket in North Salem, New York. This, along with a lack of application of my intellectual curiosity in traditional academics, lead me to culinary school at Johnson and Wales University, in Providence, Rhode Island. It turns out I liked eating but not cooking. I graduated with a degree in hotel restaurant management. While in college I worked as a bellman (among other roles) in a few different hotels.

Upon graduation from J&W, I worked my way up through the ranks in the hotel industry. Over the course of 12 years, I worked for both Marriott and a Marriott franchisee. My career in the hospitality industry provided me with the opportunity to interact with dozens of people each day. Through this experience I learned to ask good questions, listen for the answers, and most importantly, help people. In every role I held I had to develop relationships with clients. I use that knowledge every day.

My consulting career began when I received an offer to start a business from scratch with the Gallup Organization. The company had an office in New York City but wanted a native New Yorker to "push his way into CEOs' offices" (that's the way my boss described the job). I was great at selling consulting, but I didn't push people, ever. I still don't.

I went back to school and earned two master's degrees. The professors at Pace University and Columbia University treated graduate students with real-world work experience as peers. My intellectual curiosity was piqued when we solved problems in real companies.

Being struck by a taxicab on the corner of 6th Avenue and 43rd Street in New York was the best thing that ever happened to me. It was the final push I needed to start my own consulting company.

I was confident but comfortable, which led to some inconvenient exit timing from a role at Gallup that paid me well.

At age 40, I was an entrepreneur in a massive recession, with no business, and a newborn baby. I was sufficiently motivated.

Lawyers flocked to me because the way I teach selling doesn't seem like selling (one large law firm client forbade me from using the word *sales*).

Today I help business leaders develop sales strategy. I also work with sales teams, independent salespeople, executives, and professional service providers. Each day is different, and I am blessed to do what I love. I focus on three things:

1. Raising great children who appreciate the limitless opportunities in life
2. Being a great husband, family member, and friend
3. Delivering outstanding value to everyone who invests in me

Thank you for investing your time with me.
I look forward to one day hearing your story.

Dave Lorenzo
888.444.5150

If you'd like to put your business growth on the fast track, here are some ways I can help:

Sales Team Training: I develop customized programs for sales teams of all sizes. Together we assess your team's strengths and employ a blend of technology and hands-on instruction to enable sustainable, organic growth.

One-on-One Executive Coaching: Business leaders turn to me for strategic guidance on revenue growth or entering a new market. We also discuss other leadership challenges such as: managing a team of high-performing professionals, building strategic alliance partnerships, and other issues that require confidential guidance.

Dave Lorenzo's Strategic Sales Academy: This is my exclusive program for entrepreneurs and sales professionals from all over the world. In this comprehensive session we cover both strategy and tactics that will help you open doors, deepen relationships, and make more money.

Information about these opportunities is available at: DaveLorenzo.com or by calling 888.444.5150

Index

221

Women and Sexuality in China